Gustav Metzger

Gustav

Curated by Kerry Brougher and Astrid Bowron

Texts: Astrid Bowron, Kerry Brougher, Norman Rosenthal

Museum of Modern Art Oxford

Metzger

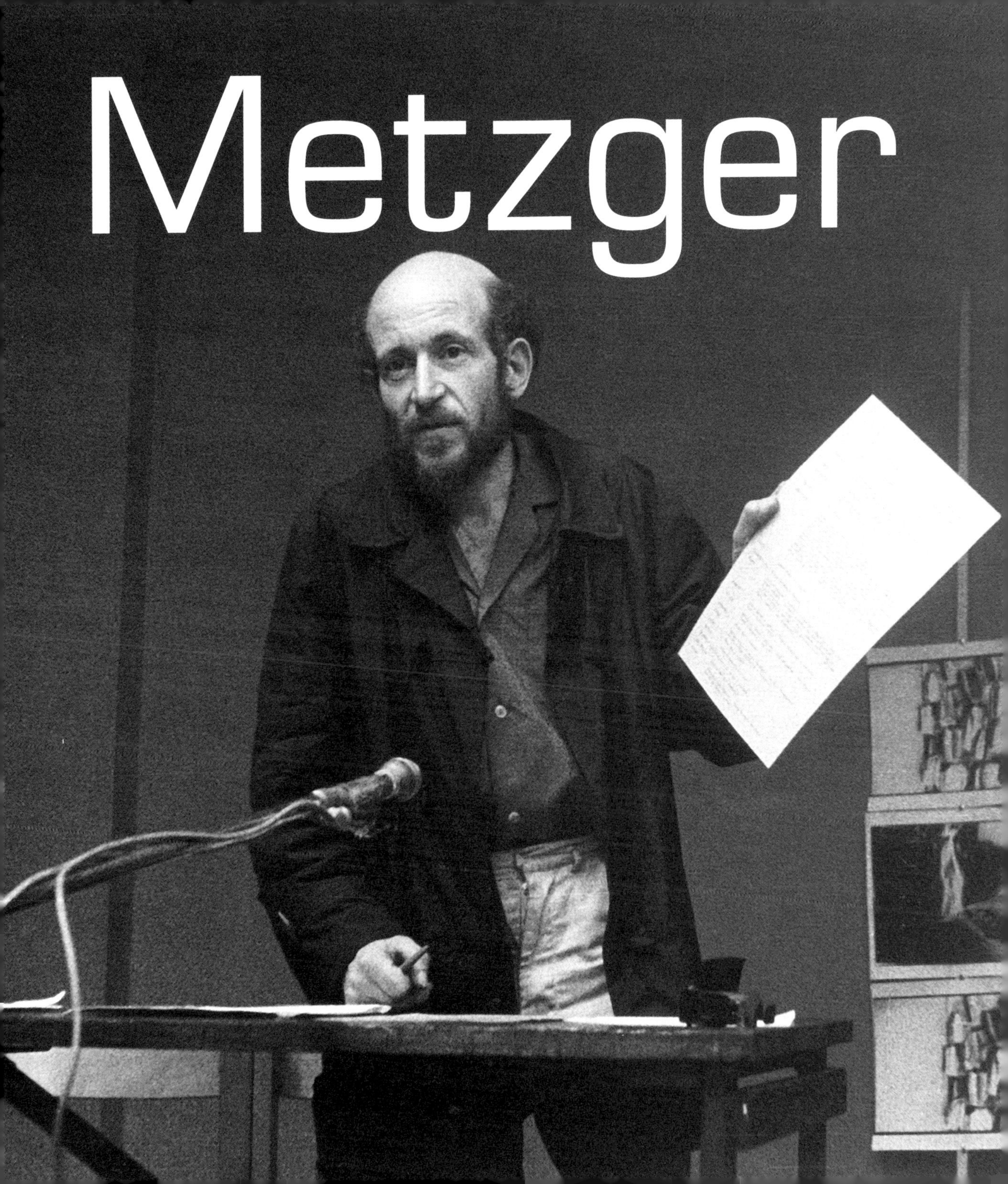

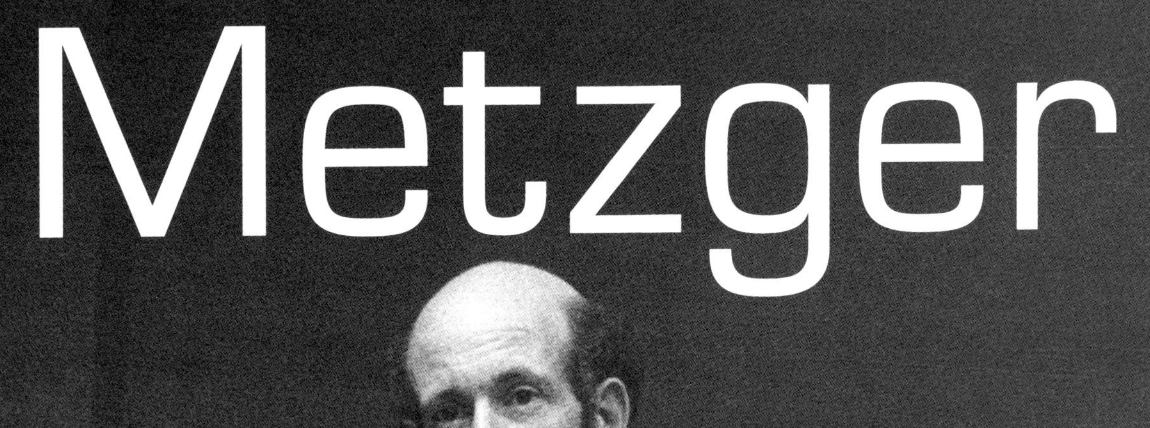

Published by the Museum of Modern Art Oxford
30 Pembroke Street, Oxford OX1 1BP
on the occasion of the touring exhibition:

Gustav Metzger
25 October 1998 – 10 January 1999

Exhibition curated by Kerry Brougher and Astrid Bowron
Publication edited by Kerry Brougher and Astrid Bowron

Designed by Herman Lelie
Typeset by Stefania Bonelli
Production co-ordinated by Uwe Kraus GmbH
Printed in Italy

ISBN 1 901352 04 8

A catalogue record of this publication is available from the British Library

Exhibition Patron: Pete Townshend.
The exhibition is supported by the ACE Live Art Commissions Fund, The Henry Moore Foundation, The John S. Cohen Foundation and The Elephant Trust.

The Museum of Modern Art Oxford receives financial assistance from the Arts Council of England and Oxford City Council.
Registered charity number 313035.

The exhibition will tour to the following venue:
Spacex Gallery, Exeter, 6 February – 20 March 1999

Additional photo credit:
photo of *Cardboards* courtesy of Andrew Wilson

Previous page:
Gustav Metzger opening the Destruction In Art Symposium (DIAS), London, September 1966

Front cover:
Liquid Cristal Slide Projections, 1998, photo: Stuart Turner

Back cover:
Caterpillar tracks, photo: Bartholomew Dudley

Contents

Foreword

Over the years, The Museum of Modern Art Oxford has developed a reputation for taking on challenging exhibitions that speak not only of aesthetic concerns but also of political and social issues. With the presentation of this survey of the work of Gustav Metzger, the Museum continues this long-standing commitment. Metzger is an artist who has remained 'at the edge' in numerous ways: in his desire to maintain an avant-garde position in his artistic activity; in his need to address the deeply disturbing social problems of the world; and in his way of life itself, a life which merges with his art and must necessarily exist at the margins, out of the grasp of corporate mechanisms and institutional power. Metzger is a genuine outsider, and as such, has been undervalued by all but a few for far too long. With this exhibition, MoMA hopes to reappraise Metzger's work and to shift it a little closer – but not too close – to the centre.

As the creator of auto-destructive art, much of Metzger's work is not merely hard to locate, it literally no longer exists. The realisation of this exhibition then has required three kinds of activity: detective work to hunt down documents and photographs of performances, demonstrations, and non-existent work; the recreation of historical work or new work in the spirit of older work; and the creation of new works. Obviously this approach necessitated a close working relationship between the artist and the many people involved in the realisation of the exhibition. Among these is Astrid Bowron, who, as my co-curator, I would like to personally thank; her commitment to Metzger's work and total dedication to this project made this exhibition a reality. We are grateful to Norman Rosenthal for sharing his personal perspective on the artist, with whom he has had a close association for many years, in his insightful essay for this book. This publication is the result of the superb efforts and talents of Herman Lelie and Stafania Bonelli. Special thanks are due to a number of individuals who shared their personal knowledge, understanding and admiration of the artist gained over the years: Ivor Davies, Adrian Glew, Justin Hoffmann, Luise Metzel, Hans Ulrich Obrist, Clive Phillpot, and Andew Wilson, among others. Thanks are also due to Paul Schimmel who first suggested a show of Metzger's work to me and Chrissie Iles, our former Head of Exhibions, who participated in early discussions about the project before her move to New York and had long been a supporter of Metzger's work.

Exhibitions of this sort are not easy to fund; therefore it is with great enthusiasm that we give special thanks to our exhibition patron, Pete Townshend. Without his generous support this exhibition would not have been possible. We are also extremely grateful to the Arts Council of England Live Art Commissions Fund, whose support has made possible a series of live events which form an integral part of this exhibition, The Henry Moore Foundation, The John S. Cohen Foundation, and The Elephant Trust.

We greatly appreciate the generosity of the lenders to the exhibition: Archiv Sohm, Staatsgalerie, Stuttgart; The Arts Council Collection; Ivor Davies; Luise Metzel and those who wish to remain anonymous. In addition we would like to thank the staff of the Tate Gallery Archive and the Wiener Library in London for their help with the research of this project.

The physical manifestation of this exhibition would not have been possible without the expert technical co-ordination of Bartholomew Dudley who, through his diligence and resourcefulness, has orchestrated a challenging exhibition installation. Many thanks are also due to those individuals who worked closely with the artist to recreate old work and construct new work: Martin Goody, Andew Paterson, Jonathon Radford, Paul Turner, and Stella Senior. The complex realisation of the Liquid Crystal Environment was made possible through the expertise and persistent efforts of Adrian Fogarty and Stuart Turner. In addition, we would like to thank those on MoMA's staff who worked particuarly hard and energetically, among them Press and Publicity Officer Tiffany Black, Head of Education Ian Cole, Head of Development Robert Moye, Development Officer Carole Scott, and Education Co-ordinator Emma Thomas. In addition, we would also like to thank Steve Morgan; The Librarian, Bishopsgate Institute, London; Walker Machinery, High Cogges, Witney; and Mattacol, London. For the most valuable support of all I would personally like to thank Nora Halpern.

Finally, we would like to thank Gustav Metzger, whose patient questioning and unwavering dedication to this project was the engine that drove it to become a reality. His concern with people and his belief in art that can potentially change the world was an inspiration for everyone involved.

Kerry Brougher
Director

A world on the edge of destruction: setting the stage for Gustav Metzger

Kerry Brougher

The artist who appears just before noon looks as if he stepped out of a First World War battlefield. Wearing a heavy jacket, gloves, and a gas mask, he offers a striking contrast to the large sheets of red, white and black nylon pulled across the rebar frame in front of him. The onlookers that have gathered at the South Bank on this summer day of 1961 watch as he lifts up a spray gun and begins to 'paint' the nylon. At first nothing happens, but a few seconds later the nylon begins to disintegrate leaving large swatches of negative space. It becomes apparent that the object being created is also simultaneously destroying itself. The man in the gas mask keeps attacking the nylon; in twenty minutes the artwork is complete – and has all but vanished.

The man who gave this acid-painting demonstration was Gustav Metzger, an artist who despite working since the fifties remains to this day an elusive figure. Metzger's peripheral position is largely due to his unwillingness to play by the established rules of an art community built on capitalist economics. Rather than supplying lasting objects and saleable goods, Metzger has focused on creating works which contain within their making the means for their destruction. The year before his South Bank performance, Metzger wrote in his second manifesto 'Auto-destructive art re-enacts the obsession with destruction, the pummelling to which individuals and masses are subjected... Auto-destructive art mirrors the compulsive perfectionism of arms manufacture – polishing to destruction point.'[1] Not only does this document, along with others written by the artist, suggest that post-war art must 're-enact' the destructive tendencies of mankind and enter into the public arena, it also indicates that the definition of art must be reconsidered and expanded. For Metzger, art is not merely objects, it is life itself; a performance, political demonstration, subversive act, intervention, lecture, manifesto – all are works of art. To understand Metzger's work we must take into account his life and the world in which he has lived. Metzger's ambitious desire to blur the lines between political engagement and artistic activity did not come out of a void; rather, it grew out of the Holocaust and developed throughout the fifties and sixties, an era that hovered in the shadow of the War and buckled under the threat of industrial-scaled destruction and nuclear annihilation. To understand Metzger's

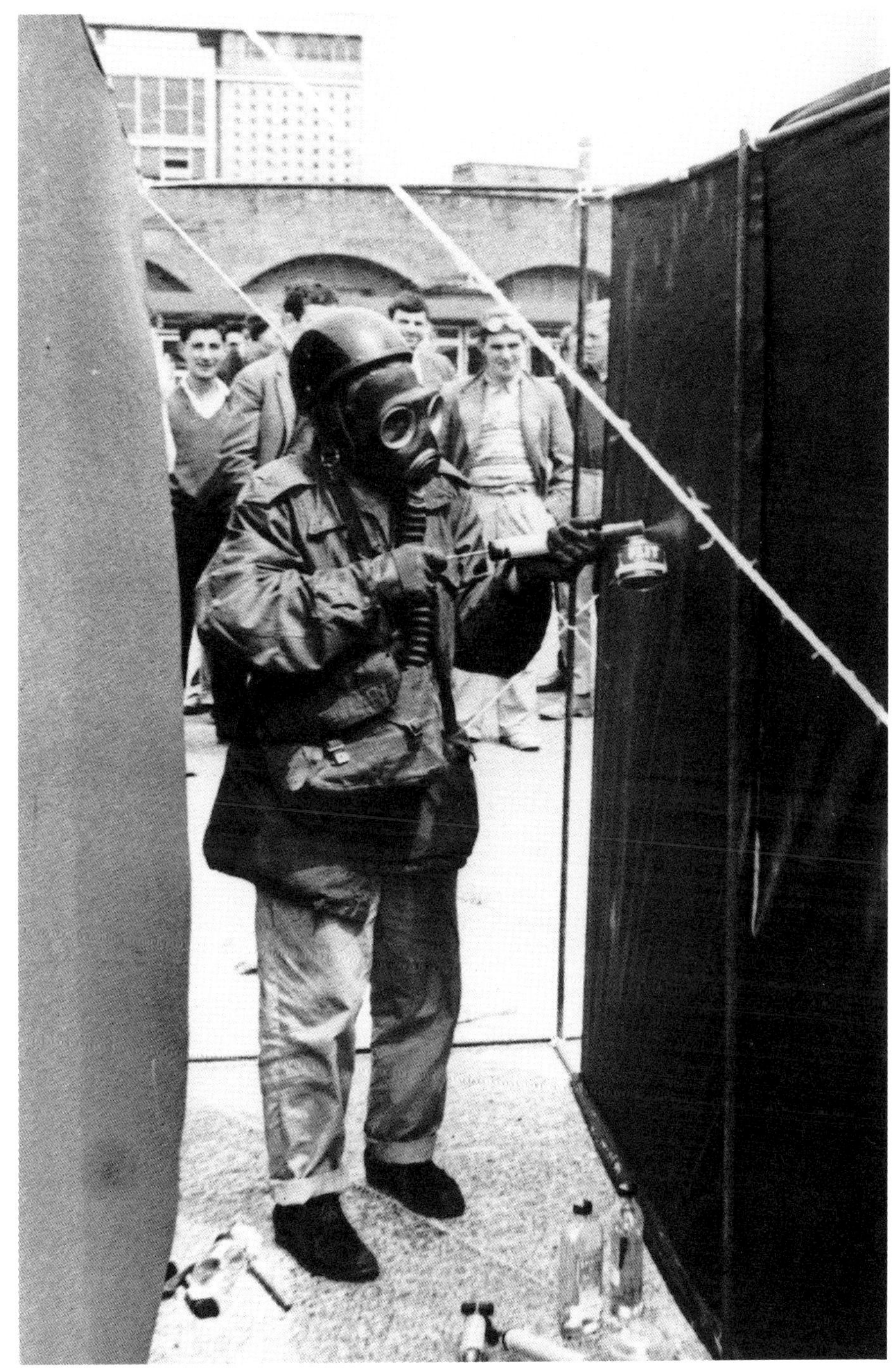

Gustav Metzger,
South Bank Demonstration,
3 July, 1961.
Photo: Hulton Getty Picture Collection

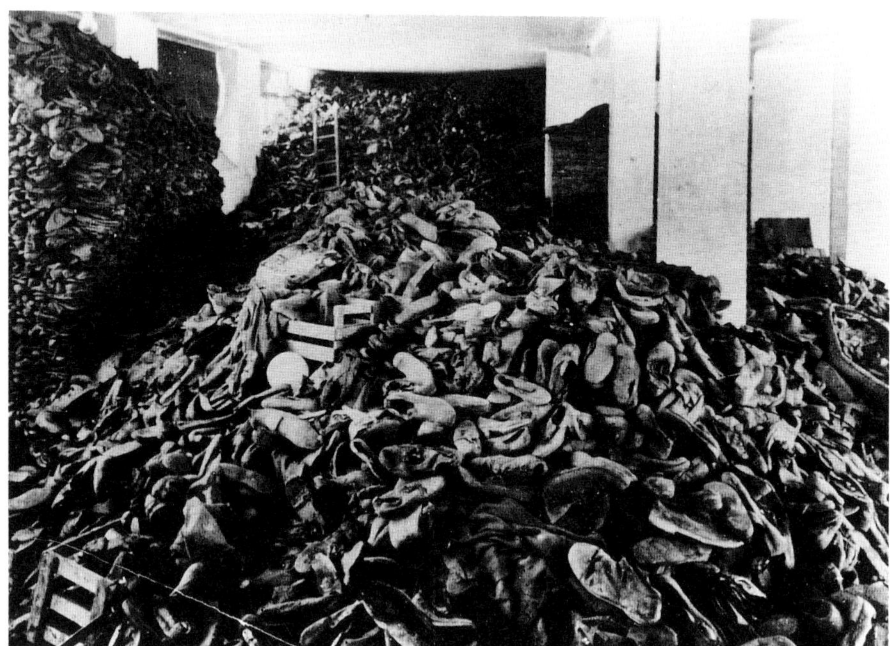

Alan Renais,
Nuit et brouillard
(Night and Fog), 1955.
Photo:
British Film Institute

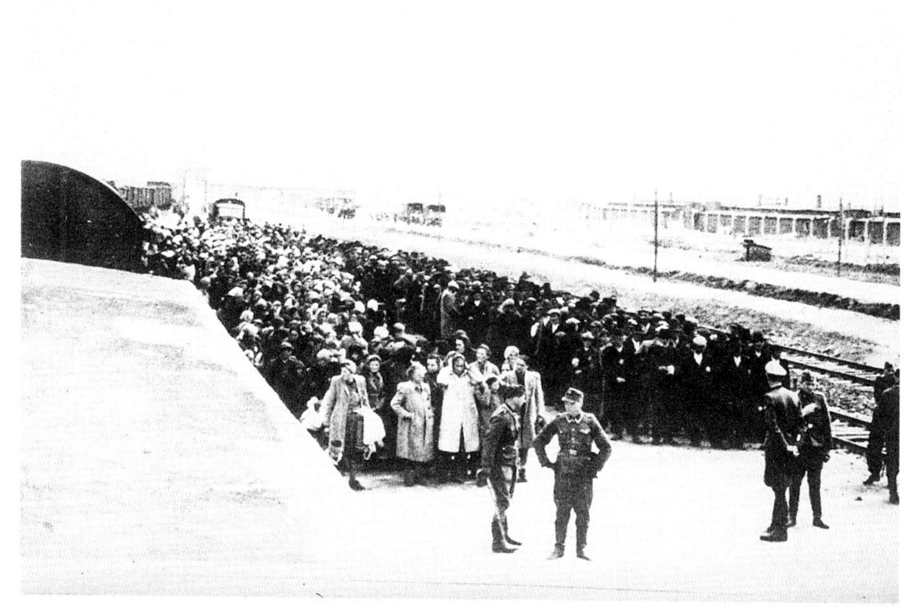

Selection,
Auschwitz,
Summer 1944

art, we must travel back in time to the Holocaust and the immediate post-war period, to an age on the eve of destruction.

The cinema is a good means of time travel, so we begin the journey by looking at a work done a few years before Metzger's South Bank performance, Alain Resnais's documentary film essay *Nuit et brouillard* (Night and Fog, 1955). Although most of the images in Resnais's film are still photographs, through the medium of cinema they take on a life, flickering, vibrating, pulsating. Yet these cinematic images are also strangely dead, for these are scenes of concentration camp life: railroad tracks and sealed freight cars, skeletons and hospital experiments, the hollow-eyed stare of men and women who have given up on life, the unbelievable ability of some men to walk among these victims oblivious to their suffering, belongings piled high, bodies piled higher. In the magical medium of film these images are no longer text book illustrations – images made to be hand-held, tossed aside at will – but still images brought back to life or at least, to a state of the undead: a camera-eye that slowly glides over the seemingly innocent green landscape of Auschwitz in 1955, and then ever so gently slides back to the grainy black and white ghosts of ten years before – a camera of the present that refuses to look away from the past.

Now imagine that this memory is inescapable, that it cannot be shut off by turning off the film projector or leaving the theatre. This is the memory of Gustav Metzger, a man who lives in the state of perpetual night and fog, an artist who must constantly interact with the nightmare of the twentieth century. Sent as a boy to England, he avoided the actual experience of the death camps, a fate not shared by his parents who died there. The most horrendous of Metzger's memories, like Resnais's film, are therefore mostly second hand, yet all too real, the black and white images quickly passed over in books and journals brought back to life in the mind's eye.

Now using this time machine, leap from 1945 to the present. We are standing in front of a new work in Metzger's recent series of *Historic Photographs*. Forced by the wall behind us to stand a bit too close to the ghostly black and white images collaged on the wall in front of us, we struggle to decipher what it is we are looking at. And what is the image? Perhaps we – like the people who are barely visible in the photograph – cannot know the truth, for we are too close to it, too much a part of the scene. Only later, when we look in a publication can we make out the entire photograph used by Metzger: the bleak landscape at the edge of Auschwitz; a ramp; two lines, one of women and children, the other of men; the SS officers overseeing this separation of families. Like Resnais's film which avoids being just a documentary, Metzger has created a situation that opens the photo back up, that removes the dust of history and the veil of the media that have long ago turned a living incident into a mere document. Metzger revives memory and once again makes it life. As we move past, we become the people in the photograph, too much a part of the scene to understand it, too human to imagine the inhumanity coming. Time has been snatched away; we are back in 1944. Metzger's work is about memory and the merging of the present and past, death and life, life and art.

The acid painting demonstrations are also a means of blurring art and life, of energising art with the same destructive potential that has infiltrated life itself in the twentieth century. As early as 1959, Metzger turned away from the traditional forms of art such as painting and sculpture and instead wrote his first manifesto on auto-destructive art. It was the end of the separation between his art and his life and the beginning of a commitment to art that would extend into every facet of his life. For Metzger, this was a necessity in the face of the possibility of mass annihilation and a society that seemed intent on self-destruction and the permanent damaging of nature. The Holocaust; Hiroshima and Nagasaki; wars in Korea, Algeria, and Indochina; the Hydrogen Bomb; the onslaught of televised images; the increasing identification with commodities; the over-production and terrible waste of capitalistic society; the polarisation of world powers; environmental pollution – the immediate post-war era was a tumultuous time in which science demonstrated its ability to create marvels of destructive potential never before imagined, leaving most people paralysed with wonder – and fear. For some people, after Auschwitz there could be no more poetry. For Metzger there could be poetry, but it had to be an art that aimed at introducing destruction as a means of 'transforming peoples' thoughts and feelings, not only about art, but to use art to change peoples' relation to themselves and society'.[2] Auto-destructive art was conceived 'as a desperate, last minute subversive political weapon... an attack on the capitalist system... an attack also on art dealers and collectors who manipulate modern art for profit.'[3]

In fact, destruction in art had been around for some time. Metzger himself informs us that auto-destructive art 'has its roots in the Dada movement, in Russian Revolutionary art 1910–1920, and in a direction, which is best represented by Moholy-Nagy.'[4] Indeed modernism itself is linked with the concept of destruction and iconoclasm, the destruction of old art to allow the rise of new art.[5] Ruins – both real and constructed – placed within the eccentric gardens and parks of the eighteenth and early nineteenth century such as Stourhead or Fountains Abbey, are among the first notions of the romanticising of decay that launches the modern period.[6] The photograph extended this desire to reclaim the past through its ruins; William Henry Fox Talbot's studies of Gothic ruins, for example, not only speak of the mystery of absence but also of modernism's desire to define itself

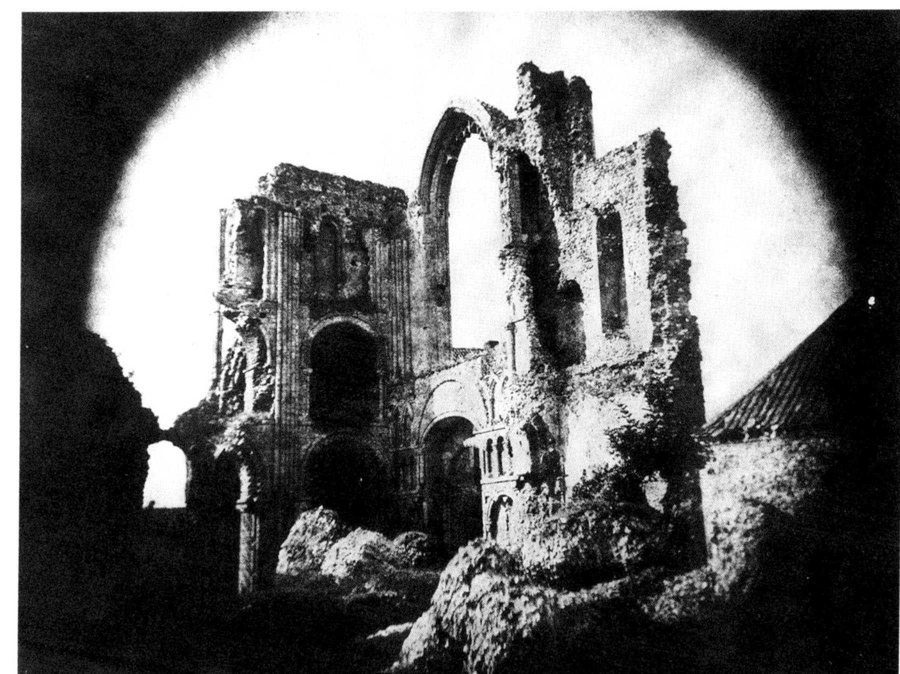

William Henry Fox Talbot, *Castle Acre Priory, Norfolk*, *c.*1845 Collection of the National Museum of Photography, Film and Television, Bradford. Photo: NMPFT/Science and Society Picture Library

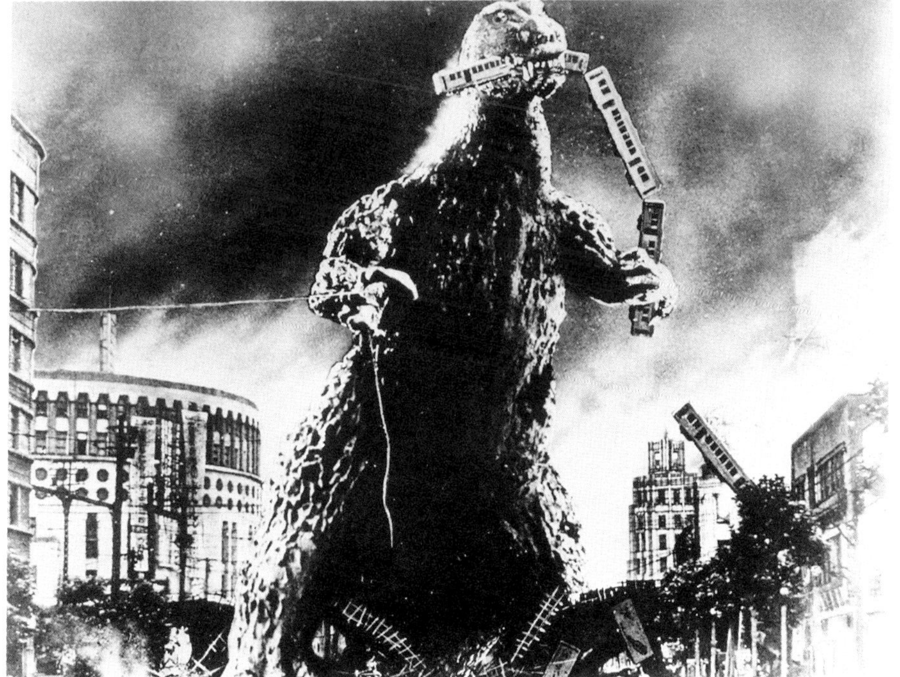

Ishiro Honda, *Godzilla*, 1954. Photo: British Film Institute

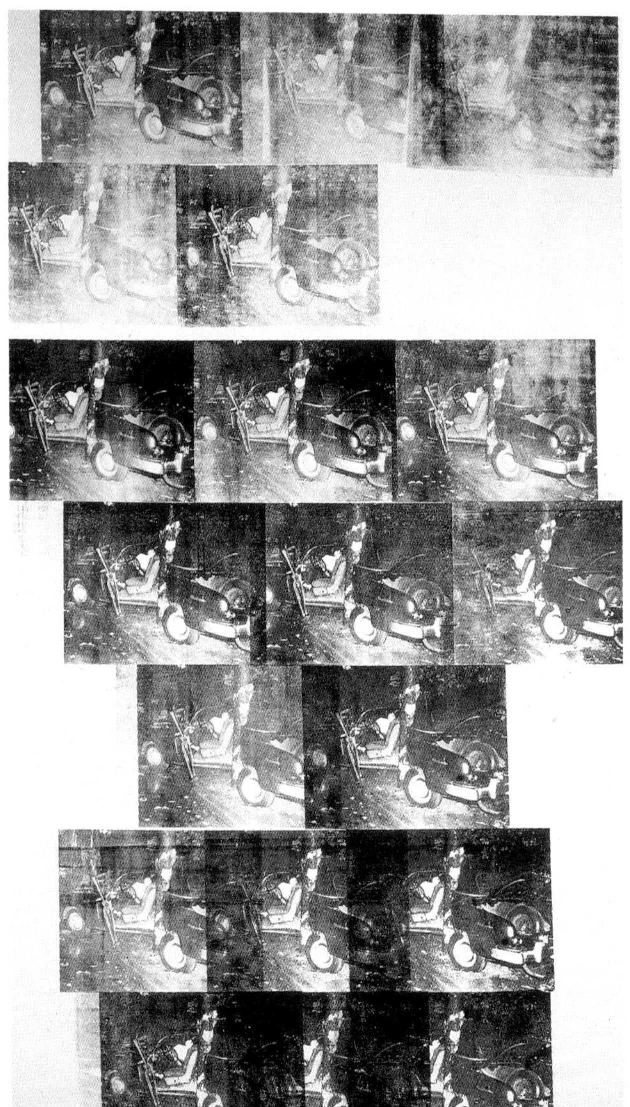

Andy Warhol, *White Car Crash Nineteen Times*, 1963
Private collection, courtesy Thomas Ammann Fine Art, Zurich.
Photo: Thomas Ammann Fine Art, Zurich

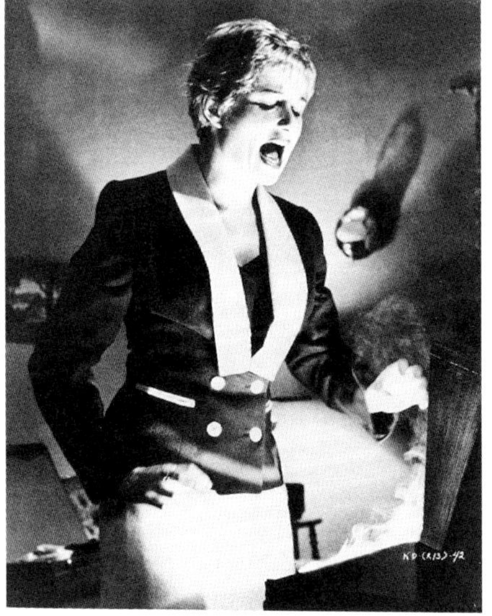

Robert Aldrich, *Kiss Me Deadly*, 1955 .
Photo: British Film Institute

by its separation from this past, a separation created by a sea of time that has left the former world in ruins. This emphasis on the break with the past continues in the twentieth century. Marinetti's Manifesto of Futurism states that 'a racing car... is more beautiful than the Victory of Samothrace' and Malevich suggests that we ignore art history and 'let all periods burn, as one dead body,' echoing the radical spirit inherent in the concept of the avant-garde.[7]

But the tendency for destruction in art takes on new urgency in the post-war period. Indeed, culture world wide, led by the cinema, seemed to recognise the dire state of mankind and the need for revealing a sickness underlying the utopianism of post-war progress. Film noir captured the sense of American paranoia in films such as Billy Wilder's *Sunset Boulevard* (1950) and Orson Welles's *Touch of Evil* (1958), while in Japan the effects of the Bomb and mankind's tampering with nature were still rumbling on in the disaster films launched by the studio Toho, such as Ishiro Honda's *Godzilla* (1954) and its sequels with their fiery destructions of Tokyo. In the finale of Robert Aldrich's *Kiss Me Deadly* (1955), science-fiction and noir meet as Mike Hammer, the hard-boiled detective, lies helplessly wounded watching as the femme fatale opens the world up to a Pandora's box of radioactive horror. Michelangelo Antonioni's films from *L'Avventura* (1960) to *Il Deserto Rosso* (1964) capture the sense of alienation in the post-war industrial wasteland while later in *Zabriskie Point* (1970) the director stages one of the cinema's most dazzling explosions – rivalled only by Stanley Kubrick's *Dr. Strangelove or How I Learned to Stop Worrying and Love the Bomb* (1964), which features found footage of atomic bomb explosions resulting in an essay on the majestic beauty of the final destruction. Not to be outdone, Andy Warhol unleashed his own painting of the Bomb in 1965 as an extension of his 'disaster' series of car crashes and electric chairs, which like Kubrick's film and Bruce Conner's assemblage film *Crossroads* (1976), repeats the blast over and over in an endless chain reaction.

But all of this was the image of destruction, not destruction itself. For many artists in the fifties and early sixties, these representations of destruction were not enough; rather, they felt the need to incorporate destructive acts right into their work, to bring destruction out of the two-dimensional world of representation into the three-dimensional space of reality. In *Manifesto Blanco* (White Manifesto, 1946), Lucio Fontana called for an art which would go beyond two dimensions and take into account the third and fourth dimension; his means of doing this was to slash the canvas. Like Jackson Pollock, Fontana saw painting as action, but unlike Pollock he literally broke through the canvas, overcoming abstract painting's inability to avoid being a representation; for as radical as Malevich or Mondrian had been, a red square could still be read as, well, the image of a red square. Fontana's act of slicing the canvas transformed fictive space into real space, two-dimensions into three dimensions, the conventional window onto another world into the physical material of this world. Nor were these 'rebellious' acts confined to Fontana; in Japan, Shozo Shimamoto built up canvases with papered surfaces only to puncture them with a series of holes and Saburo Murakami created large paper panels which he would then destroy by jumping through them with his own body. Back in Italy, Mimmo Rotella created a series of décollages by tearing layer after layer of posters off buildings while in Germany Günther Uecker was driving nails into the surface of the work. In Paris, Yves Klein used a blowtorch and the co-operation of the fire department to create his series of *Fire Paintings*. On a more sculptural scale Korean composer and artist Nam June Paik manipulated both pianos and televisions to subvert their conventional usage, Swiss artist Jean Tinguely made a machine which collapsed in front of New York's Museum of Modern Art, and Raphael Montañez Ortiz smashed and chopped up furniture and pianos in a series of 'therapeutic' performances. Soon these destructive acts were extended to the audience and the artist's own body; in Yoko Ono's *Cut Piece* the audience was invited to cut the dress off her body while Viennese Actionists such as Günter Brus, Hermann Nitsch, Otto Muehl, and Rudolf Schwarzkogler were involved with Dionysian 'materialaktions' that included outrageous orgies of destructive debasement. The various movements which encompass these approaches to art – *Nouveau réalisme*, the Gutai Group, Viennese Actionism – all seem to share the desire to use destructive tendencies to overcome the burden of history and collective guilt.[8]

These actions point out the schizophrenic nature of the fifties and early sixties. While *Leave It to Beaver* dominated American television and presented the perfect family unit, films such as Don Siegel's *Invasion of the Body Snatchers* (1956) were reminding everyone that dark forces somewhere out there could overtake America at any time. While Ortiz smashed his pianos and Otto Muehl created a film with Kurt Kren in which a woman given an enema defecates on the artist's body, America ate TV dinners and the world drank Coke. It was an era of tinfoil and Geiger counters, Disney Homes of Tomorrow and bomb shelters, Atom Age progress and Atom Age devastation.

The world was in a state of rapid, uncontrollable transformation, edging ever closer to the abyss but pretending that science was creating a better tomorrow. Artists began to tap into these modernist neuroses. Self-destruction became part of the process of creation, whether it was Niki de Saint Phalle shooting at her paintings or Wolf Vostell's use of a locomotive to destroy a Mercedes Benz. In the process of doing this, these artists were building not only on their Dada heritage but also on a lineage of modernism that runs from Manet through Duchamp and up to Pollock, a lineage that marries form and content with an emphasis on

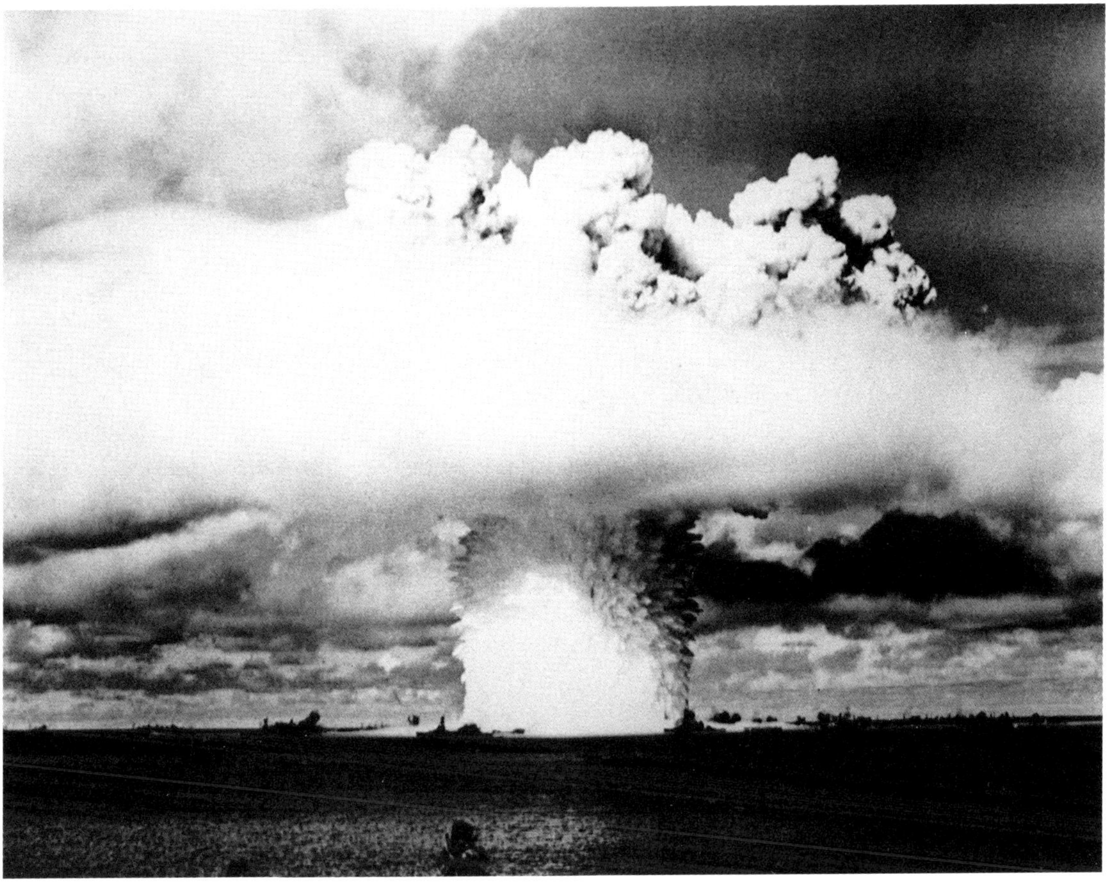

Bruce Conner, *Crossroads*, 1976 .
Photo: Anthology Film Archives, New York

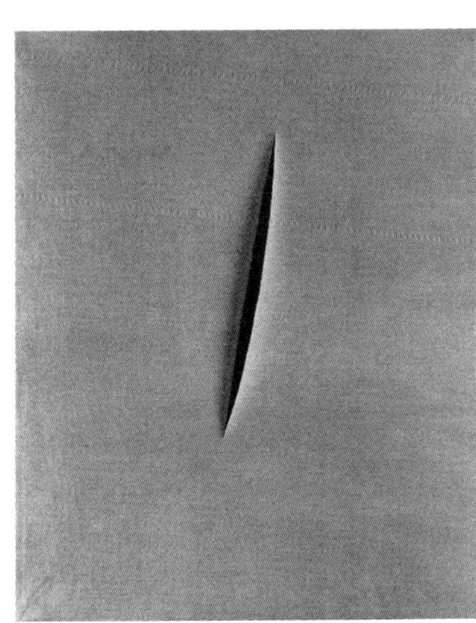

Lucio Fontana,
Concetto Spaziale 'Attessa', 1960
Collection of the Tate Gallery, London.
Photo:
Tate Gallery, London

process. This approach, which privileges the formless over the geometrically structured and emphasises such qualities as the material itself, liquid states, entropy, base materials, and the operation or process, seems to be used, along with its interest in the subversion of the viewer's expectations, to give expression to a kind of modern neurosis. What these works have in common is the lack of an expected form and content resulting in an unclassifiable state, an aesthetics of revulsion, an overriding interest in the body, and a sense that the work is in the state of constant transformation, even on the verge of disappearing.[9]

Metzger's acid paintings clearly fall within this arena. Formless, nearly non-existent twenty minutes after their making, they are simultaneously markers of neuroses and a cathartic process to overcome these neuroses. As such they could be seen not only as a groping for power from the destructive potential of post-war technology, but also as an operation to help rebuild the patient – the patient being the artist, the spectator, and society itself. Indeed, Metzger himself has stated the need for a balance to auto-destruction; in 1961 he wrote a manifesto that included the concept of 'auto-creative art,' an 'art of change, movement, growth.'[10] Perhaps the most significant outgrowth of auto-creative art was Metzger's liquid crystal light projections for such rock groups as The Who and Cream in 1966. The burst of colour created by heating liquid crystal on glass slides and then projecting them onto the walls and performers creates a situation in which the forms 'in transformation have an effect on the automatic nervous system.'[11] Like the proto-hallucinogenic experiments of the fifties and early sixties such as the Vortex Concerts at the Morrison Planetarium in San Francisco; John and James Whitney's Zen-inspired, computer-derived abstract films; the Stargate Corridor sequence from Kubrick's *2001: A Space Odyssey* (1968); Stan Brakhage's epic film *Dog Star Man* (1961–64), or Jordan Belson's 'cosmic' films, Metzger's liquid crystal projections were designed as a means of inducing change by offering a mythic, expansive view of the world that attempted to neutralise the neurotic tendencies inherent in modern life and offer an alternative consciousness. Simultaneously, with their constantly changing surface, one colour transforming into another, one shape into another, Metzger's liquid crystal projections are also auto-destructive; they are never static but always in flux, a liquid state in perpetual motion, caught between coolness and heat, an artwork that is objectless, containerless, and formless.

Perhaps auto-destructive art has had a part in the shaping of our current world view. In a recent video interview Metzger told Hans Ulrich Obrist that he felt 'we are becoming more realistic. We're facing up to the dangers of the technology – thirty years ago we didn't do that... There was so much uncertainty, there was so much disclarity – about everything.'[12] Metzger's nightmare, his pessimistic view of a world gone mad and on the brink of destruction, which was launched by the Nazis over fifty years ago and filtered through the technological phobias of the fifties and sixties and the ravaging of nature in the seventies and eighties, is perhaps finally on the verge of destroying itself – the black and white images of Auschwitz, the ghosts of the past, giving way slowly, ever so slowly, to the colours of the present.

1
Gustav Metzger, 'Manifesto Auto-Destructive Art', 1960, reprinted in Gustav Metzger, *Damaged Nature, Auto-Destructive Art*, Coracle @ workfortheeyetodo, London, 1996, p. 59.

2
Metzger, *Damaged Nature, Auto-Destructive Art*, p. 27.

3
Gustav Metzger Quoted in John Walker, 'Message from the Margin, John A. Walker tracks down Gustav Metzger', Art Monthly, no. 190, October 1995, p.15.

4
Metzger, *Damaged Nature, Auto-Destructive Art*, p. 25.

5
See Dario Gamboni, *The Destruction of Art: Iconoclasm and Vandalism since the French Revolution*, Reaktion Books Ltd, London, 1997, pp.255–286.

6
See Michael S. Roth, *Irresistible Decay: Ruins Reclaimed*, with essays by Claire Lyons and Charles Merewether, The Getty Research Institute for the History of Art and the Humanities, Los Angeles, 1997.

7
Quoted in Gamboni, p.259.

8
See Paul Schimmel, 'Leap into the Void: Performance and the Object' in *Out of Actions: Between Performance and the Object, 1949–1979* (ex. cat.), Russell Ferguson (ed.), Museum of Contemporary Art, Los Angeles and Thames and Hudson, New York, 1998.

9
See Yve-Alain Bois and Rosalind E. Krauss, *Formless: A User's Guide*, Zone Books, New York, 1997, originally published in France as *L'Informe: mode d'emploi*, Editions du Centre Pompidou (ex. cat.), 1996.

10
Gustav Metzger, 'Auto-Destructive Art, Machine Art, Auto-Creative Art', manifesto, 23rd June, 1961.

11
Gustav Metzger, 'Auto-Destructive Art', manifesto, reprinted in Metzger, *Damaged Nature, Auto-Destructive Art*, p.54.

12
Gustav Metzger in 'Hans Ulrich Obrist Interviews Gustav Metzger', transcription of a video interview, 19 September, 1997, London, unpublished, unpaginated.

Gustav Metzger

Astrid Bowron

There is no easy way to understand the career of an artist whose works have for the most part only temporarily if ever existed. Gustav Metzger's art has comprised a staggering array of publications, actions, lecture-demonstrations and manuscripts, most of which have only in the later years of his life been catalogued,[1] a few of which have been recorded on film or photographs but most of which have eluded any form of visual documentation.

For Gustav Metzger, ideas formed out of a lifelong pre-occupation with politics and social issues, a critique of the capitalist system and the desire for social change, are the very focus of his art. What sets him apart from other artists are the high ideals which he has set himself, ideals which have excluded him from mainstream circulation. His is a life in which art and politics have become totally merged and such are the complexity and interdisciplinary nature of his activities that he must resist any form of easy categorisation. Any attempt to unravel Gustav Metzger the artist must come through a combined look at his own personal history, including the tragic events of his early life, and an examination of his life's work, the connections and inter-relatedness of which have powerfully come full circle with the work he has done in recent years.

Formative Years

Gustav Metzger was born in Nürnberg in 1926, the youngest son of a Jewish Orthodox family of five children. Both his parents were Polish immigrants and his father ran a specialist Jewish grocery business in Nürnberg, notorious centre for the Nazi rallies. As the Nazis underwent their persecution of the Jewish people, Metzger, then twelve, and his elder brother Max (later known as Mendel), were sent to Britain as Polish citizens under the auspices of the Refugee Children movement. His parents did not survive the Holocaust.

Upon arrival in England in January 1939, Metzger and his brother were initially housed for a brief time in Butlins Holiday Camp, then in a hostel for refugee children in London, and were eventually evacuated to Hemel Hempstead at the outbreak of war. In September 1941 Metzger started a three year course to train to be a cabinet-maker in Leeds which ended after a year because of the War. It was in

Leeds that he first encountered the work of Henry Moore, Graham Sutherland, Matthew Smith, Jacob Epstein, Paul Nash, Barbara Hepworth, John Piper, and Gaudier-Brzeska. He started working as a furniture maker in 1942, and became interested in revolutionary left-wing politics, reading Communist literature and the writings of Eric Gill. In 1943 and 1944 he worked for six months at the Harewood Estate and became a vegetarian. In 1944 he moved to Bristol and lived in a commune of Trotskyists and Anarchists in a villa in Clifton, while he worked on farms outside the city. It was through Derek Eastmond, a visitor to the commune that he became familiar with the work of Wilhelm Reich.

It was in the August of that year that Gustav Metzger decided to become a sculptor instead of a professional revolutionary, and whilst working in the organic garden at Champneys nature-cure clinic near Tring, he started carving his own sculptures with small pieces of stone. Later that autumn, at the National Gallery he met Henry Moore and asked him if he could work as the artist's assistant. Moore's advice instead was that he should start by going to art school to study life-drawing. It was by chance, in that same year that he also met for the first time, Eduardo Paolozzi in the Ashmolean Museum in Oxford.

Taking Moore's advice to heart, Metzger studied full and part-time at various art schools in Cambridge, London, Antwerpen and Oxford including the Sir John Cass Institute in Aldgate East where he studied sculpture and drawing from 1945 until the summer of 1948. In 1945 and 1946 Metzger himself worked as a life model and also attended other life drawing classes which led to his significant meeting with David Bomberg who was teaching the evening life class at the Borough Polytechnic. The painter Bomberg, who was himself Jewish, was to play a profoundly influential role on Metzger's development. In the winter of 1946 Bomberg encouraged Metzger to begin painting in the daytime composition class and recommended him for a grant which would enable him to study full time. At this time, Metzger began to form his own ideas about painting which he thought should be 'fast and intense'.

Metzger also began work on a monumental carving of 'a two-figure theme' on a blitzed site opposite the Sir John Cass Institute, the hard stone block coming from a bomb-damaged building. He studied with the sculptor Bainbridge Copnall and with Nicholas Egon who taught the technique of painting and the history of art. Significantly, it was Egon who first pointed out the connection between art and science which was to remain an enduring fascination for him for the rest of his life. In the years that followed, Metzger was to spend many hours in the British Museum Library increasing his knowledge by reading up on such subjects as embryology. In the next few years Metzger also extended his interests in other art forms such as dance and theatre, notably with classic Indian dance and music, and formed friendships with Mollie Pitts and Michael Bullock.

The heat of the summer of 1947 forced Metzger's artistic activity to be confined to the indoors of his East End studio shack where he swapped carving outdoors for painting with his own self-mixed paints. In 1948 he exhibited a large painting he had made the previous year at a group show at the Ben Uri Art Gallery, and subsequently at the London Group exhibition at the Academy Hall in London from 21 May to 6 June.

That year he obtained a stateless passport which enabled him to travel to the Netherlands, Belgium and France to study European painting and build up connections, such as with the family of Van Gogh with whom he discussed making a film about Van Gogh's late painting *Crows over a Cornfield*. With the aid of a grant from the Jewish Community of Antwerpen, this study tour was extended into three terms of full-time art studies, which enabled him to study drawing and painting under Gustaav de Bruyne at the Koninklijke Academie voor Schoone Kunsten in Antwerpen. From there he traveled to Paris and Nice.

In 1949 he returned to England, attending the Oxford School of Art and then Central School of Art in London. The Haendler Trust grant was extended for a further year on the recommendation of Jacob Epstein. In London he resumed his evening classes at the Borough Polytechnic (until the summer of 1953). He showed three paintings at the Whitechapel Art Gallery in the exhibition *East End Academy* from 3 September to 14 October 1950.

1951 was the year of the Festival of Britain and Metzger made repeated visits to the Festival site. In the summer he toured Scotland and later began working as a casual labourer on the land and on building sites which occupied him on and off until 1953. He took a studio near Mornington Crescent in London, which was later passed on to Leon Kossoff and Frank Auerbach. He lent his support to David Bomberg in his plan to establish a school in Spain. In the spring of 1953 he wrote to Douglas Cooper and Herbert Read and began to write on Bomberg.

In this year Metzger was instrumental in the forming of the 'Borough Bottega' and he exhibited in the group exhibition *Drawings and Paintings by the Borough Bottega* at the Berkeley Galleries in London. In December, Metzger resigned from the group and David Bomberg broke off his relations with him in a letter.

King's Lynn: Turning Points in Art and Politics

In the December of 1953 Metzger moved to King's Lynn in Norfolk where he worked as a junk dealer. Although based in King's Lynn he made frequent visits to London where he was profoundly struck by one exhibition in particular held at the Whitechapel Gallery from 9 August to 9 September 1956. The exhibition that he has described to Andrew Wilson as 'one of the deepest art experiences of my life'[2] was *This is Tomorrow*, often considered the first exhibition of British Pop Art. He has estimated that he visited this exhibition at least six times and in a show of support Metzger staged his own exhibition of posters of some of these artists in the window of a King's Lynn shop that he had hired.

Later that year, again in the empty shop space, he organised a modest exhibition of sculptures by Eduardo Paolozzi, William Turnbull and Anthony Hatwell who had been a fellow student of Bomberg's. This was also prompted by *This is Tomorrow* in which Paolozzi had participated, but also by Metzger's personal association with him. Metzger wrote about the event for the local press which was his first published article.

The next exhibition Metzger was to organise was of old church art for the King's Lynn Festival of 1957, but it was to be other, more politically motivated events of that year which changed the course of his life and his work. He became a founder member of the King's Lynn Committee for Nuclear Disarmament when the Campaign for Nuclear Disarmament was in the very early stages of its development. He remained partially active with the group until 1958 by supporting the Direct Action Committee Against Nuclear War (DAC) in its first rocket base campaign and later, in December of that year, he participated in the two supporting marches for the rocket base occupations in North Pickenham.

However, a more significant event in terms of his personal and artistic development came in the autumn of 1957. He had heard that there were plans for major redevelopment of the old King's Lynn fishing quarter and in protest he single-handedly launched the North End Protest against redevelopment of this ancient quarter of the town, a protest which led to the formation of the North End Society, of which he became secretary. The event was covered extensively by the local press, and in so doing, brought the cause to the attention of local dignitaries. Metzger's confidence grew when he realised that committed action against what he perceived as being injust and inhumane actions could actually have an effect. This gradual 'radicalisation' of Metzger gave him the courage to fly in the face of public scrutiny and not be afraid to take bold, isolated action where he deemed it necessary, and signalled a dramatic turning point in his work.

From this point forth, Metzger's life was to be a constant balance between art and political activism. Throughout these politically active two years, Metzger had also kept up with new developments in art, following with keen interest the completion of Alison and Peter Smithson's New Brutalist school in Hunstanton, near King's Lynn and continuing to make frequent visits to exhibitions in London, notably the Kurt Schwitters exhibition at the Lords Gallery in 1958, and the second Schwitters show there eight months later.

Cardboards and the First Manifesto, 1959

In 1959 Metzger took part in the Aldermaston March and in the summer of that year he moved back to London where three of his paintings were exhibited in the basement coffee shop at 14 Monmouth Street, near Leicester Square run by a young kinetic artist, Brian Robins. However, it was his later exhibition of *Cardboards* at 14 Monmouth Street from 9 to 30 November, and the writing of his first manifesto, *Auto-Destructive Art*, dated 4 November 1959, that signalled the change of his work as an artist, from painting to something radically different, an art that was taken literally from the real world around him and which seemed to herald the legacy of other vanguard art forms, notably Duchamp's readymades, Dada, Russian Constructivism and modernist architecure. What made Metzger's proposal for a new art form so different was that its original components had to be 'machine made' found objects that would be for 'temporary usage', and undergo transformation over a period of time.

For the *Cardboards* piece, Metzger selected six pieces of used cardboard packaging, probably from a television set, and situated them as a group against the white gallery wall. The manifesto document, presented as a plain typed sheet, in what was to prove a typically understated style of presentation for all his manifestos, could not have been more in contrast to the radical nature of the document's content.

The manifesto contains a statement on the *Cardboards* in which Metzger proclaims that 'These cardboards are nature unadulterated by commercial considerations or the demands of the contemporary drawing room./ They have reference to the greatest qualities of modern painting, sculpture and architecture./ These cardboards were made automatically for a strict purpose and for a temporary usage.'

John Cox photographed the event and Metzger gave a telephone interview with John Rydon for the *Daily Express*. The article that appeared in the newspaper the next morning with the headline 'Bearded man trips over a box and finds a new form of art... IT'S PICTURES FROM PACKING CASES' was predictably sceptical in a good-humoured way but, nevertheless, recognised that the artist's intent was a serious one and made his activities known to a much wider public.[3] The photograph and story were syndicated around the world and appeared in at least three other international publications.

On 20 October 1996, Metzger wrote another statement about this piece which co-incided with his making a new version of the *Cardboards* in an installation for the exhibition *Made New: Barry Flanagan, Tim Mapston, Gustav Metzger, Alfred Jarry*, at City Racing, London, from 25 October to 17 November, curated by Andrew

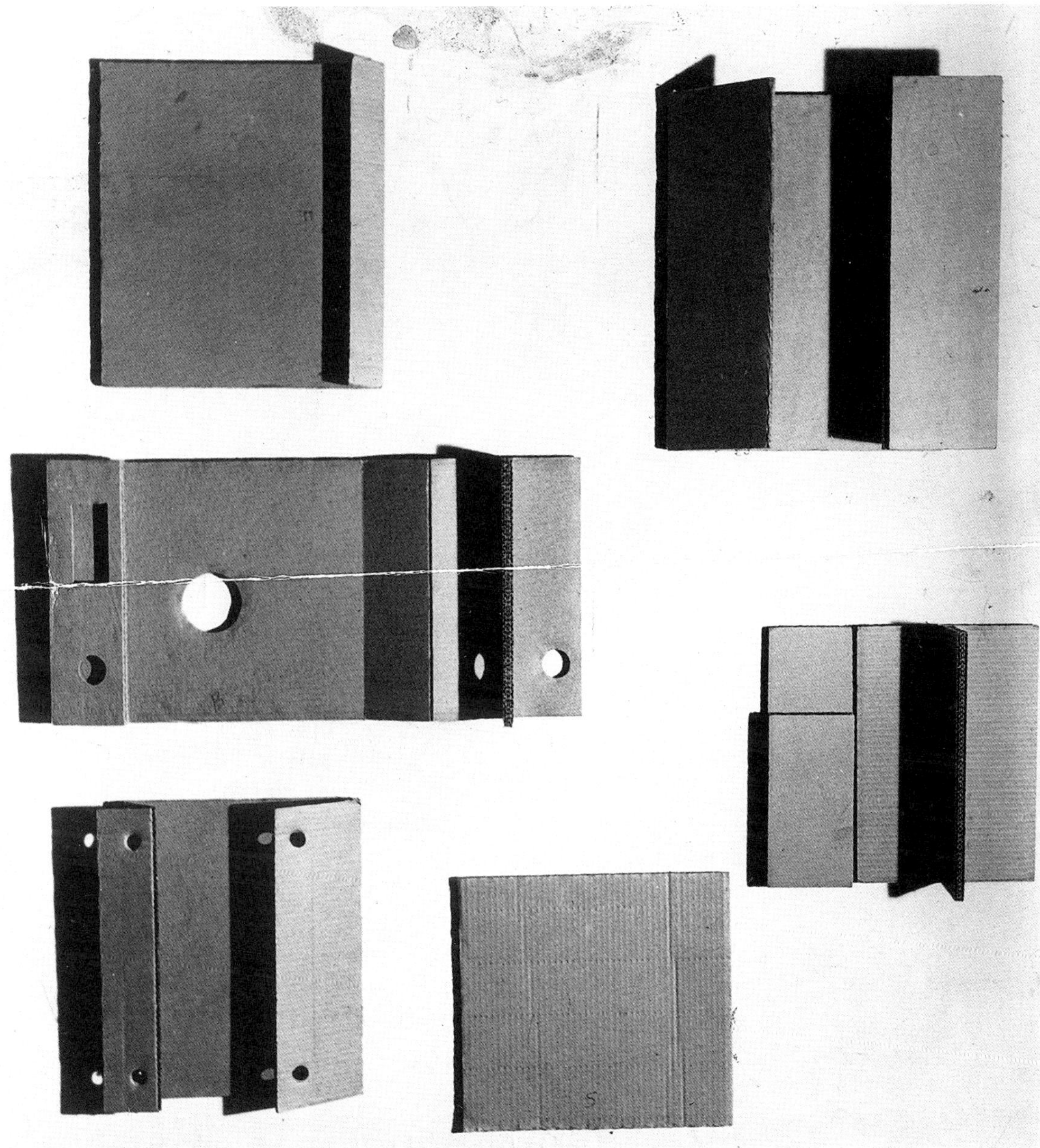

Cardboards exhibition at 14 Monmouth Street, London, November 1959.
Photo: John Cox (Ida Kar Studio)

Cardboards selected and arranged by G. METZGER at 14 Monmouth Street, W.C.2, near Cambridge Circus

The discarded cardboard which is on view was probably part of a television package.
These cardboards are nature unadulterated by commercial considerations or the demands of the contemporary drawing room.
They have reference to the greatest qualities in modern painting, sculpture and architecture.
These cardboards were made automatically for a strict purpose and for a temporary usage.

A U T O D E S T R U C T I V E A R T

Auto-destructive art is primarily a form of public art for industrial societies.

Auto-destructive painting, sculpture and construction is a total unity of idea, site, form, colour, method and timing of the disintegrative process.

Auto-destructive art can be created with natural forces, traditional art techniques and technological techniques.

The artist may collaborate with scientists, engineers.

Auto-destructive art can be machine produced and factory assembled.

Auto-destructive paintings, sculptures and constructions have a life-time varying from a few moments to twenty years. When the disintegrative process is complete the work is to be removed from the site and scrapped.

London, 4th November, 1959 G. METZGER.

~~The ... of~~ The amplified sound of the auto-destructive process can be an integral part of the total conception.

The cardboards are on view from Monday 9th-30th November.
Open daily from 6 p.m. to midnight.

The exhibition will open quietly at 6 p.m. Monday 9th November.

Statement on *Cardboards* and First Manifesto: *Auto-Destructive Art*, 1959

Bearded man trips over a box and finds a new form of art

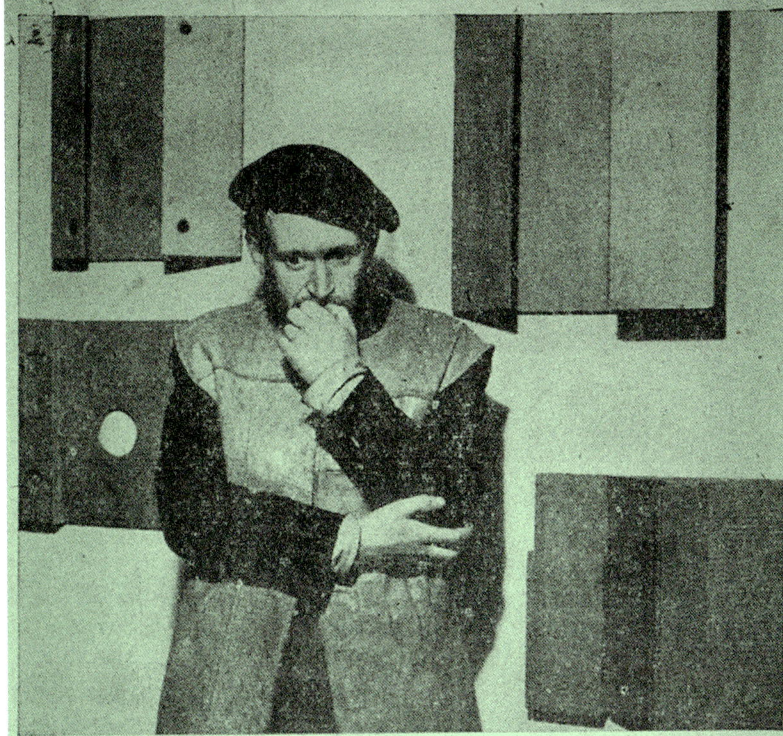

"Cardboarder" Gustav Metzger yesterday—and some of his works

IT'S PICTURES FROM PACKING CASES

By

JOHN RYDON

A LONDON artist, who considers old cardboard boxes have qualities equal to the greatest in modern painting, is showing his first exhibition of "machine-made art."

He is bearded, 33-year-old Gustav Metzger, German-born abstract artist, who discovered his new "art" when he fell over a packing-case for a TV set in a shop doorway three months ago.

Mr. Metzger told me last night: "I took the packing case to pieces and thought of using them as decorations for my room.

"These carboards are nature unadulterated by commercial considerations or the demands of the contemporary drawing-room."

I stumbled down a precipitous staircase into basement premises in Monmouth-street, Holborn, where a whole wall was taken up with the Metzger "work." Geometrical slabs of cardboard packaging, some with holes in them, hung from nails.

Went on Mr. Metzger: "I don't want to sell any of these; (a) because I like them so much I want to keep them; and (b) since there must be a large supply of similar material lying around I don't want to prevent other people getting it free too.

"I'm thinking of making a big collection of these cardboards with the aim of having a really BIG show. I've never seen anything quite like it."

I said I hadn't either.

Mr. Metzger continued: "I should like to have the chance of turning these into architectural decorations. You move them in any way you like.

"There is an inherent harmony and artistic quality in all of them."

Then the ex-joiner who has studied at art schools in Britain and the Continent asked whether I was interested in hearing his theory of "auto-destructive art."

I said I had heard enough.

John Rydon's article on the *Cardboards* exhibition, November 1959 in the *Daily Express* with a photograph by John Cox

Wilson. The new statement reflected Metzger's changing ideas towards the piece which he saw as having a new relevancy in the 'real' world some thirty seven years later: 'Cardboards, cardboard boxes, are for us now inextricably linked to fraught figures seeking shelter in cities; the present showing re-emphasises the social content of – cardboards.'[4]

First Manifesto: Auto-Destructive Art, 1959

Although Metzger had written the first manifesto document, he not only credits Brian Robins as contributing to the statement on the *Cardboards*, but also in persuading him to adopt the term Auto-Destructive Art instead of Self-Destructive Art which had been his original intention. Metzger agreed that this new term was not only more dramatic but much more evocative of the spirit of the art that it proposed. However, neither Robins or any of the other artists associated with 14 Monmouth Street followed Metzger along the path to auto-destructive art by putting their name to the manifesto and no movement as such was ever formed. The manifesto statement *Auto Destructive Art*, however, was to become the theoretical basis of all of Metzger's activity and in adhering to its principles, again he faced isolation, this time in his artistic convictions, a state in which he was to remain for a long time after.

On 12 November of that year Metzger attended a cyclomatic event and lecture by Jean Tinguely at the ICA London. Tinguely continued to be a figure of major interest to Metzger.

Second Manifesto: Manifesto Auto-Destructive Art, 1960

On 10 March 1960, Metzger published an updated version of his first manifesto which included the hand-written addition 'The amplified sound of the auto-destructive process can be an integral part of the total conception' which became the fourth line of the original statement.[5] The new document was presented, again as one single sheet, with his second manifesto, *Manifesto Auto-Destructive Art*, beneath it.

Metzger presented his first model for an auto-destructive sculpture in the *Daily Express* two days before Jean Tinguely's *Homage to New York* at the Museum of Modern Art, New York on 17 March 1960.

In June of that year Metzger returned to his King's Lynn studio to develop a technique for painting with acid on nylon. He experimented with a form of action painting that involved applying acid with brushes to a nylon sheet laid on a board about which John A. Walker has noted 'the slashed canvases of Lucio Fontana, the self-destroying machines of Jean Tinguely and the fire paintings of Yves Klein were comparable developments... Auto-destrucive art was conceived as a 'desperate, last minute subversive weapon... an attack on the capitalist system... It is committed to nuclear disarmament... It is an attack also on art dealers and collectors who manipulate modern art for profit'.[6] John Cox took photographs which were published, together with Metzger's statement, for *Art and Artists* in August 1966.

First Lecture/Demonstration, 1960

Metzger gave his first Lecture/Demonstration *Auto-Destructive* Art at the Temple Gallery in London on 22 June 1960. This was a live performance comparable with the contemporaneous Happenings of the New York based artists Allan Kaprow and Yoko Ono. During the event which was introduced by Jasia Reichard, he painted an auto-destructive acid 'action' painting on nylon with a brush, his face unprotected against the acid. The effects of the acid made the nylon peel away and dissolve before his and his audience's very eyes. He had mastered what he has come to call many times since, an 'aesthetic of revulsion'.

At this event Metzger had also displayed his first model, as well as found objects: machine made forms, cardboards, and a paper and fabric-filled polythene bag. Some walls were plastered with the day's newspapers in what Metzger has described as 'a display of total visual chaos'. This first utilisation of newspapers is a significant detail for newspapers were to remain a constant and enduring fascination for Metzger and a rich source of material for his work throughout the rest of his career. As found objects, they represented the world's physical 'reality' to Metzger, but taken literally, encompassed a more global reality.

In September, also at the Temple Gallery, Metzger had a one person exhibition, *Paintings and Drawings 1945–1960* but this did not include the acid nylon painting (*Acid on Glass*), for he felt it was inappropriate to show it in a commercial gallery setting. He did in fact later show the acid nylon painting there to Lucio Fontana, who had an exhibition in the McRoberts Gallery in October to November of that year.

In October 1960, Metzger gave a Lecture/Demonstration at the Heretics Society, Trinity College, Cambridge organised by Ian Sommerville. The large audience included William Burroughs and Brion Gysin. All the walls were covered in that day's Sunday newspapers.

That same year, Metzger became a founder member of the anti-nuclear war Committee of 100 which were a group of people willing to commit acts of civil disobedience in order to provoke and overwhelm the authorities. Other members included the philosopher Bertrand Russell.

AUTO DESTRUCTIVE ART

Auto-destructive art is primarily a form of public art for industrial societies.

Self-destructive painting, sculpture and construction is a total unity of idea, site, form, colour, method and timing of the disintegrative process.

Auto-destructive art can be created with natural forces, traditional art techniques and technological techniques.

The amplified sound of the auto-destructive process can be an element of the total conception.

The artist may collaborate with scientists, engineers.

Self-destructive art can be machine produced and factory assembled.

Auto-destructive paintings, sculptures and constructions have a life time varying from a few moments to twenty years. When the disintegr-ative process is complete the work is to be removed from the site and scrapped.

London, 4th November, 1959 G. METZGER

MANIFESTO AUTO-DESTRUCTIVE ART

Man in Regent Street is auto-destructive.
Rockets, nuclear weapons, are auto-destructive.
Auto-destructive art.
The drop drop dropping of HH bombs.
Not interested in ruins, (the picturesque)
Auto-destructive art re-enacts the obsession with destruction, the pummelling to which individuals and masses are subjected.
Auto-destructive art demonstrates man's power to accelerate disintegr-ative processes of nature and to order them.
Auto-destructive art mirrors the compulsive perfectionism of arms man-ufacture - polishing to destruction point.
Auto-destructive art is the transformation of technology into public art. The immense productive capacity, the chaos of capitalism and of Soviet communism, the co-existence of surplus and starvation; the increasing stock-piling of nuclear weapons - more than enough to destroy technolo-gical societies; the disintegrative effect of machinery and of life in vast built-up areas on the person,...

Auto-destructive art is art which contains within itself an agent which automatically leads to its destruction within a period of time not to exceed twenty years.
Other forms of auto-destructive art involve manual manipulation. There are forms of auto-destructive art where the artist has a tight control over the nature and timing of the disintegrative process, and there are other forms where the artists control is slight.
Materials and techniques used in creating auto-destructive art include: Acid, Adhesives, Ballistics, Canvas, Casting, Clay, Combustion, Com-pression, Concrete, Corrosion, Cybernetics, Drop, Elasticity, Electricity, Electrolysis, Electronics, Explosives, Feed-back, Glass, Heat, Human Energy, Ice, Jet, Light, Load, Mass-production, Metal, Motion, Motion Pic-ture, Natural Forces, Nuclear energy, Paint, Paper, Photography, Plaster, Plastics, Pressure, Radiation, Sand, Solar energy, Sound, Steam, Stress, Terra-cotta, Vibration, Water, Welding, Wire, Wood.

London, 10th March, 1960 G. METZGER

Manifesto Auto-Destructive Art, 1960. Courtesy of the Archiv Sohm, Staatsgalerie, Stuttgart

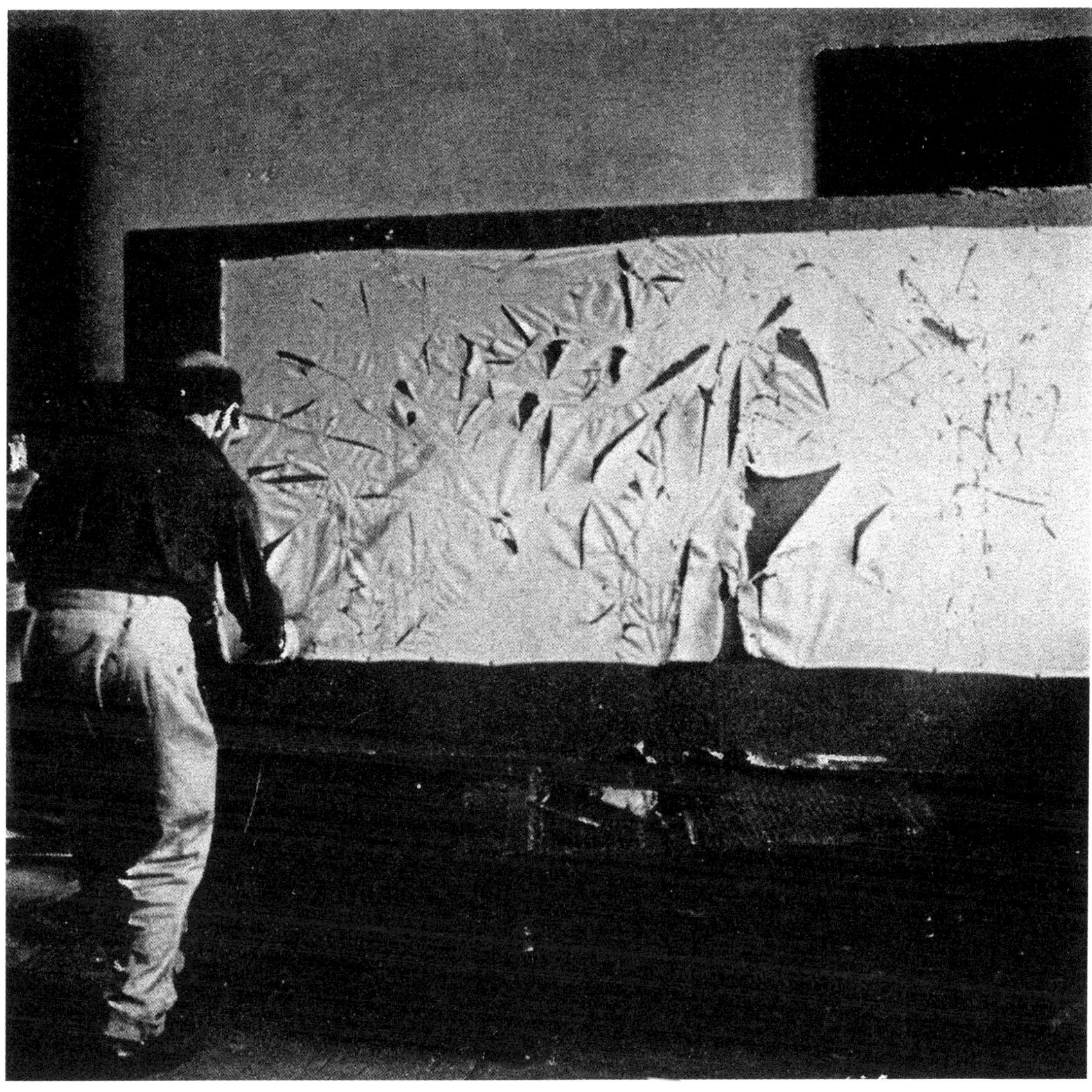

Gustav Metzger in his King's Lynn studio preparing for the first Lecture/Demonstration of June 1960. Photo: John Cox

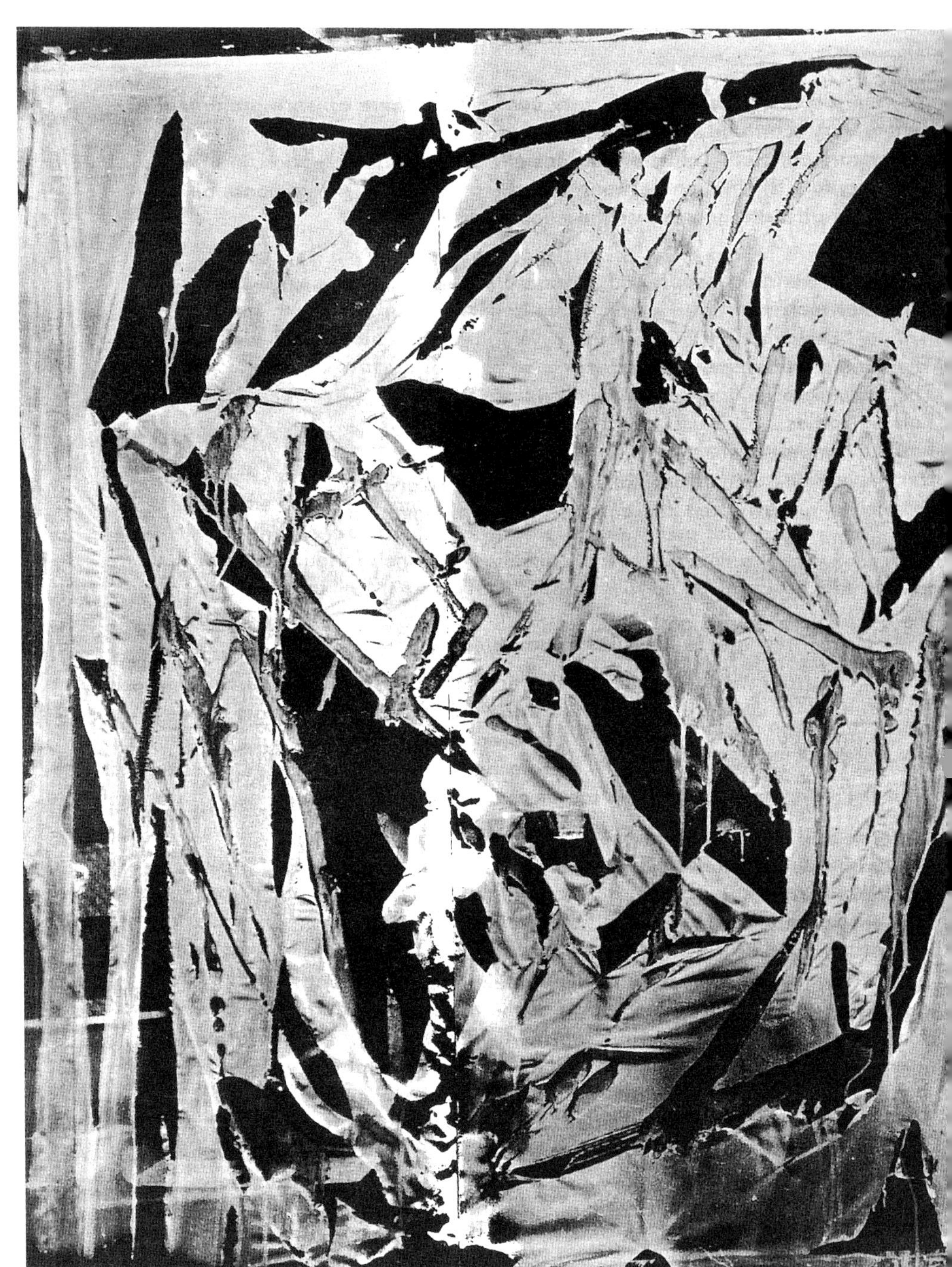

End phase of first Lecture/Demonstration: *Auto-Destructive Art* at the Temple Gallery, London, June, 1960. Photo: Cyril Wilson

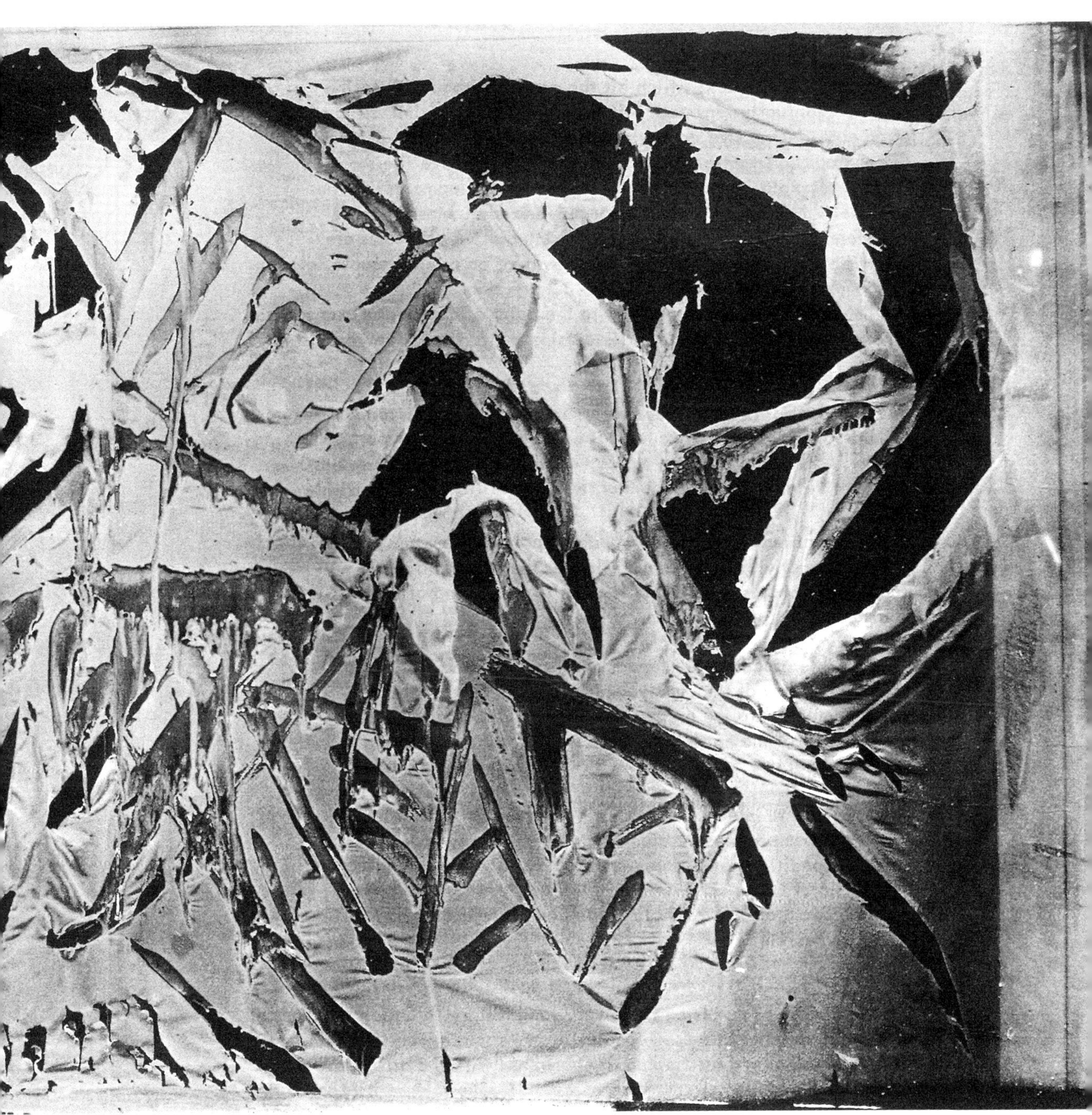

The South Bank Demonstration and Third Manifesto, 1961

On 3 July 1961, Metzger gave a demonstration of auto-destructive art at the South Bank, London. For this demonstration Metzger sprayed hydrochloric acid onto three sheets of nylon coloured white, black and red, stretched across a metal frame. As the acid made contact with the nylon, the nylon gradually disintegrated, and dissolved completely within twenty minutes. As John A. Walker put it 'The work was creative but at the same moment destructive. It also exemplified transformation over time and randomness.'[7] He also presented an auto-destructive mobile made of sheets of glass which were suspended from strings which Metzger cut in sequence, bringing the glass crashing to the ground, an event which proved potentially hazardous with the strong winds of the South Bank. Twelve assistants, most of which were students from the AA, helped Metzger with the demonstration. A press photographer took pictures of the whole event.

Metzger had produced his third printed manifesto for distribution at the event: *Auto-Destructive Art, Machine Art, Auto Creative Art*. He had timed the event to coincide with the opening of the International Union of Architects Congress which took place on that very site. The manifesto, of which 1000 copies were made, had originally included a reference to the IUA Congress but when the congress organisers refused to officially acknowledge Metzger's event, Metzger printed a black line over the wording in which the reference was made which appeared on the surface to be an integral part of the design (although the wording is still decipherable on original copies of the manifesto). This manifesto was significant in that for the first time, it directly positioned auto-destructive art as a critique of the capitalist system with the words 'auto-destructive art is an attack on capitalist values and the drive to nuclear annihilation'.

The third manifesto also introduced a new term, 'Auto creative art', which Metzger saw as the pendant to auto-destructive art, but it was not until some years later that he put these ideas into practice with his *Light Projections*, first shown in 1965 and the kinetic sculptures he made for the exhibition *Extremes Touch: Material/Transforming Art* as part of the Swansea Arts Festival in 1968.

On 12 September Metzger was jailed for a month for his participation in the Committee of 100 demonstrations. 50 members of the Committee were summoned to appear at Bow Street Court, London and out of the 37 that appeared, 32, including Bertrand Russell, refused to be bound over to keep the peace, and were imprisoned for up to two months. The court hearing was reported in *The Guardian* on 13 September, and in *Peace News*.

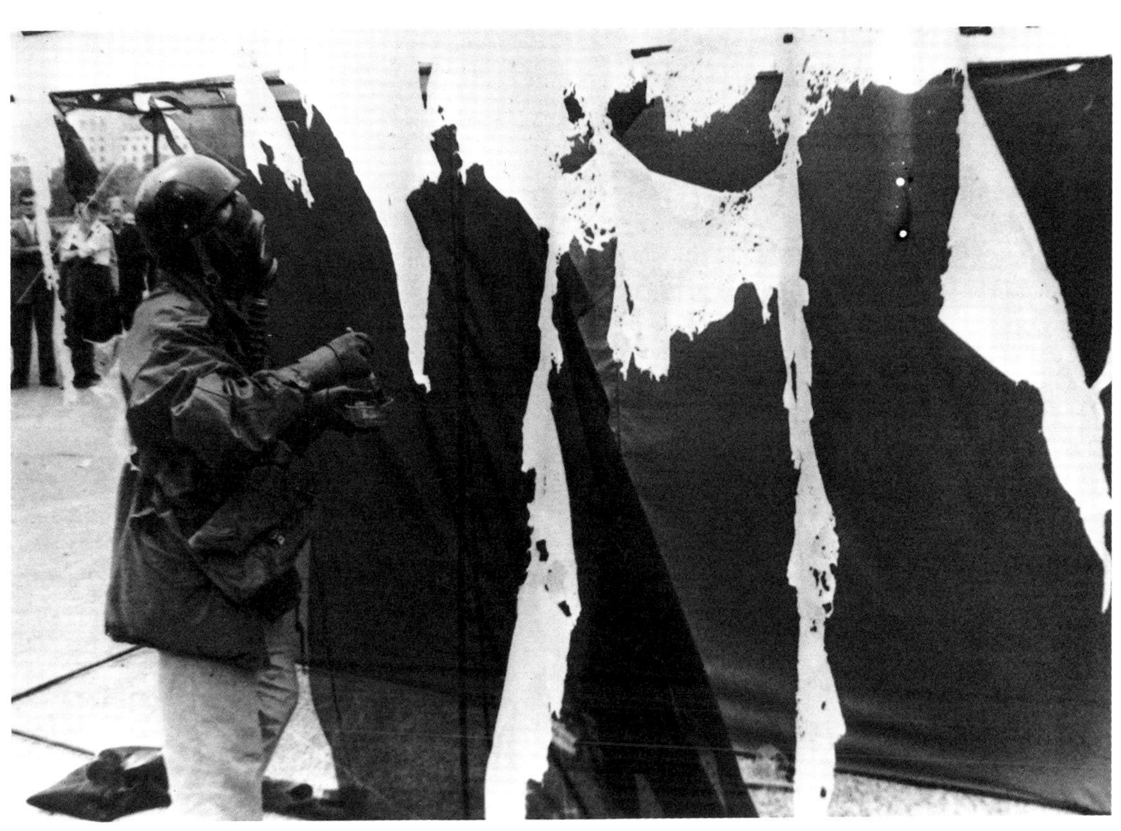

South Bank
Demonstration,
3 July, 1961.
Photo: Hulton Getty
Picture Collection

Festival of Misfits, the Daily Express and the Fourth Manifesto, 1962

Metzger was invited to participate in the *Festival of Misfits*, a group exhibition organised by Daniel Spoerri, at Victor Musgrave's Gallery One in London from 23 October to 8 November 1962. Although his participation had been advertised, his proposal, which was to do a piece displaying two copies of a day's edition of the *Daily Express* newspaper from cover to cover plastered against one wall, was rejected by the organisers who felt that the idea was not accessible enough to the general public. The days in question covered a very significant period of contemporary history, the Cuban missile crisis. However, more importantly, he did participate in the Misfits evening event which was the first Fluxus event ever to take place in Britain, at the Institute of Contemporary Arts in London on 24 October. It was here that he distributed copies of his fourth manifesto, *Manifesto World*. The manifesto, of which no known copies remain, opened with the words 'everything everything everything everything. A world on edge of destruction', a reference which could be applied to the dismal global 'reality' that is contained within the phenomena of the newspaper. The choice of the *Daily Express* was made largely because he felt that at the time it was the most interesting newspaper from a typographical perspective. This piece was never to be realised until 1997 when it was shown at the Kunstraum, München, in an exhibition of Metzger's work. For the exhibition in Oxford, Metzger is planning a new version of *Daily Express;* two front pages showing different editions of the same day's newspaper, dated Wednesday 24 October 1962. Although superficially similar, they record slightly differing versions of the previous day's events, the first 1pm edition headline proclaiming: 'HERE'S THE EVIDENCE' with a photograph taken from the sky of a Cuban missile site which resulted in the Cuban blockade; the 3pm edition's headlines reading 'THE EVIDENCE' with a new column recording the previous two hour's developments: '1am: Let's meet and talk'; an hour by hour record of history as it was being made.

Lecture Demonstration at Ealing, December 1962

1962 was a very important year for Metzger's theoretical development. He published his first article, 'Machine, Auto-Creative, & Auto-Destructive Art' in *Ark, Journal of the Royal College of Art* (London) in the summer and in December 1962, Roy Ascott invited him to give his first lecture at an art school, the Ealing School of Art. The resulting lecture/demonstration, *Auto-Destructive Art, Auto-Creative Art: The Struggle for the Machine Arts of the Future*, included fifty slides showing

AUTO - DESTRUCTIVE ART

Demonstration by G. Metzger

SOUTH BANK LONDON 3 JULY 1961 11.45 a.m.—12.15 p.m.

Acid action painting. Height 7 ft. Length 12½ ft. Depth 6 ft. Materials: nylon, hydrochloric acid, metal. Technique. 3 nylon canvases coloured white black red are arranged behind each other, in this order. Acid is painted, flung and sprayed on to the nylon which corrodes at point of contact within 15 seconds.

Construction with glass. Height 13 ft. Width 9½ ft. Materials. Glass, metal, adhesive tape. Technique. The glass sheets suspended by adhesive tape fall on to the concrete ground in a pre-arranged sequence.

AUTO-DESTRUCTIVE ART

Auto-destructive art is primarily a form of public art for industrial societies.

Self-destructive painting, sculpture and construction is a total unity of idea, site, form, colour, method and timing of the disintegrative process.

Auto-destructive art can be created with natural forces, traditional art techniques and technological techniques.

The amplified sound of the auto-destructive process can be an element of the total conception.

The artist may collaborate with scientists, engineers.

Self-destructive art can be machine produced and factory assembled.

Auto-destructive paintings, sculptures and constructions have a life time varying from a few moments to twenty years. When the disintegrative process is complete the work is to be removed from the site and scrapped.

London, 4th November, 1959 — *G. METZGER*

MANIFESTO AUTO-DESTRUCTIVE ART

Man in Regent Street is auto-destructive.
Rockets, nuclear weapons, are auto-destructive.
Auto-destructive art.
The drop drop dropping of HH bombs.
Not interested in ruins, (the picturesque)
Auto-destructive art re-enacts the obsession with destruction, the pummelling to which individuals and masses are subjected.
Auto destructive art demonstrates man's power to accelerate disintegrative processes of nature and to order them.
Auto-destructive art mirrors the compulsive perfectionism of arms manufacture—polishing to destruction point.
Auto-destructive art is the transformation of technology into public art. The immense productive capacity, the chaos of capitalism and of Soviet communism, the co-existence of surplus and starvation; the increasing stock-piling of nuclear weapons—more than enough to destroy technological societies; the disintegrative effect of machinery and of life in vast built-up areas on the person,...

Auto-destructive art is art which contains within itself an agent which automatically leads to its destruction within a period of time not to exceed twenty years. Other forms of auto-destructive art involve manual manipulation. There are forms of auto-destructive art where the artist has a tight control over the nature and timing of the disintegrative process, and there are other forms where the artist's control is slight.
Materials and techniques used in creating auto-destructive art include: Acid, Adhesives, Ballistics, Canvas, Clay, Combustion, Compression, Concrete, Corrosion, Cybernetics, Drop, Elasticity, Electricity, Electrolysis, Electronics, Explosives, Feed-back, Glass, Heat, Human Energy, Ice, Jet, Light, Load, Mass-production, Metal, Motion Picture, Natural Forces, Nuclear energy, Paint, Paper, Photography, Plaster, Plastics, Pressure, Radiation, Sand, Solar energy, Sound, Steam, Stress, Terra-cotta, Vibration, Water, Welding, Wire, Wood.

London, 10 March, 1960 — *G. METZGER*

AUTO-DESTRUCTIVE ART MACHINE ART AUTO CREATIVE ART

Each visible fact absolutely expresses its reality.

Certain machine produced forms are the most perfect forms of our period.

In the evenings some of the finest works of art produced now are dumped on the streets of Soho.

Auto creative art is art of change, growth movement.

Auto-destructive art and auto creative art aim at the integration of art with the advances of science and technology. The immidiate objective is the creation, with the aid of computers, of works of art whose movements are programmed and include "self-regulation". The spectator, by means of electronic devices can have a direct bearing on the action of these works.

Auto-destructive art is an attack on capitalist values and the drive to nuclear annihilation.

23 June 1961 — *G. METZGER*

B.C.M. ZZZO London W.C.1.

Printed by St. Martins' Printers (TU) 86d, Lillie Road, London, S.W.6.

Third Manifesto: *Auto-Destructive Art, Machine Art, Auto Creative Art*, 1961. Courtesy of the Archiv Sohm, Staatsgalerie, Stuttgart

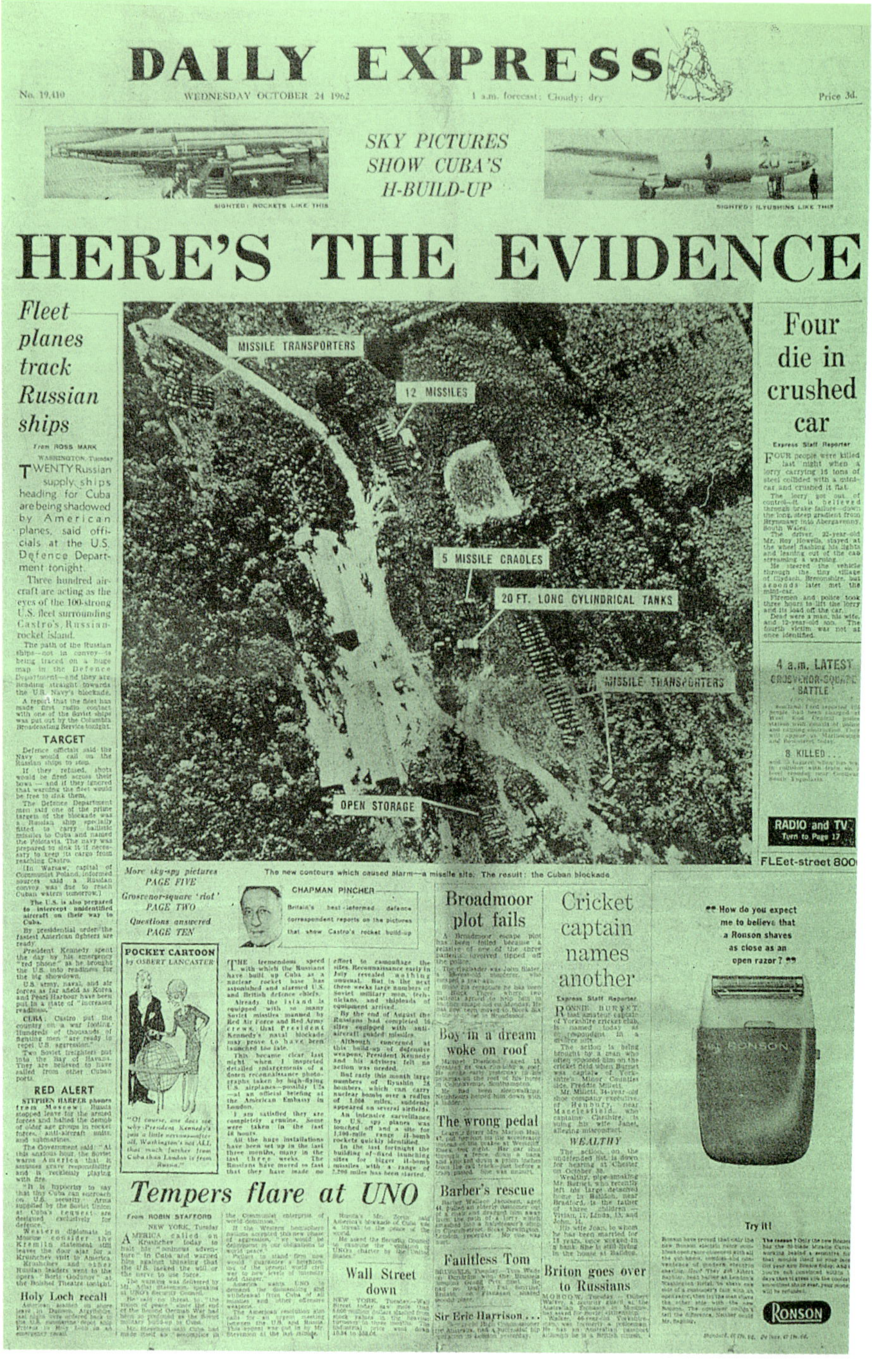

DAILY EXPRESS

No. 19,410 WEDNESDAY OCTOBER 24 1962 1 a.m. forecast: Cloudy: dry Price 3d.

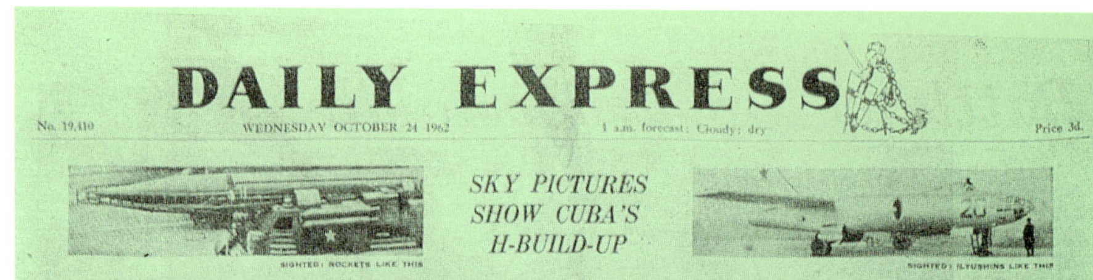

SIGHTED: ROCKETS LIKE THIS

SKY PICTURES SHOW CUBA'S H-BUILD-UP

SIGHTED: ILYUSHINS LIKE THIS

HERE'S THE EVIDENCE

Fleet planes track Russian ships

From ROSS MARK

WASHINGTON, Tuesday

TWENTY Russian supply ships heading for Cuba are being shadowed by American planes, said officials at the U.S. Defence Department tonight.

Three hundred aircraft are acting as the eyes of the 100-strong U.S. fleet surrounding Castro's Russian-rocket island.

The path of the Russian ships—not in convoy—is being traced on a huge map in the Defence Department—and they are heading straight towards the U.S. Navy's blockade.

A report that the fleet has made first radio contact with one of the Soviet ships was put out by the Columbia Broadcasting Service tonight.

TARGET

Defence officials said the Navy would call on the Russian ships to stop.

If they refused, shots would be fired across their bows — and if they ignored that warning the fleet would be free to sink them.

RED ALERT

Holy Loch recall

MISSILE TRANSPORTERS

12 MISSILES

5 MISSILE CRADLES

20 FT. LONG CYLINDRICAL TANKS

MISSILE TRANSPORTERS

OPEN STORAGE

The new contours which caused alarm—a missile site. The result: the Cuban blockade

More sky-spy pictures PAGE FIVE

Grosvenor-square 'riot' PAGE TWO

Questions answered PAGE TEN

POCKET CARTOON by OSBERT LANCASTER

CHAPMAN PINCHER

Britain's best-informed defence correspondent reports on the pictures that show Castro's rocket build-up

THE tremendous speed with which the Russians have built up Cuba as a nuclear rocket base has astonished and alarmed U.S. and British defence chiefs.

Already the island is equipped with so many Soviet missiles manned by Red Air Force and Red Army crews, that President Kennedy's naval blockade may prove to have been launched too late.

This became clear last night when I inspected detailed enlargements of a dozen reconnaissance photographs taken by high-flying U.S. airplanes—possibly U2s—at an official briefing at the American Embassy in London.

Tempers flare at UNO

From ROBIN STAFFORD

Four die in crushed car

Express Staff Reporter

FOUR people were killed last night when a lorry carrying 15 tons of steel collided with a mini-car and crushed it flat.

The lorry got out of control—it is believed through brake failure—down the long, steep gradient from Brynmawr into Abergavenny, South Wales.

The driver, 22-year-old Mr. Roy Howells, stayed at the wheel flashing his lights and leaning out of the cab screaming a warning.

He steered the vehicle through the tiny village of Clydach, Breconshire, but seconds later met the mini-car.

Firemen and police took three hours to lift the lorry and its load off the car.

Dead were a man, his wife, and 12-year-old son. The fourth victim was not at once identified.

4 a.m. LATEST GROSVENOR-SQUARE 'BATTLE'

8 KILLED...

RADIO and TV Turn to Page 17

FLEet-street 8000

Broadmoor plot fails

Boy in a dream woke on roof

The wrong pedal

Barber's rescue

Faultless Tom

Wall Street down

Sir Eric Harrison...

Cricket captain names another

Express Staff Reporter

WEALTHY

Briton goes over to Russians

Gustav Metzger, *Daily Express*, 1962/98

DAILY EXPRESS

No. 19,410 WEDNESDAY OCTOBER 24 1962 3 a.m. forecast: Dry; some sunshine Price 3d.

PICTURES FROM THE SKY SHOW CASTRO'S BIG BUILD-UP OF H-ROCKETS

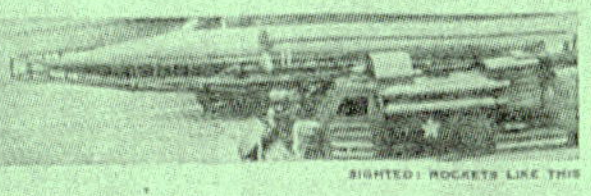

SIGHTED: ROCKETS LIKE THIS

THE EVIDENCE!

Fleet planes track Russian ships

From ROSS MARK and DAVID ENGLISH Washington, Tuesday

ARMED boarding parties of U.S. navymen and Marines are ready to search 25 Russian ships heading for Cuba, said Mr. Robert MacNamara, the Defence Secretary, tonight.

The Soviet ships are being shadowed by 300 U.S. planes acting as the eyes of the 100-strong American fleet surrounding Castro's Russian-rocket island.

Mr. MacNamara said a further 25 Russian ships are moving away from Cuba and 10 or 12 are still in port there.

The path of the ships approaching Cuba—they are not in convoy—is being traced on a huge map in the Defence Department and they are heading straight towards the U.S. Navy's blockade.

TARGET

Defence officials said the navy would call on the Russian ships to stop.

If they refused, shots would be fired across their bows — and if they ignored that warning the fleet would be free to sink them.

The Defence Department men said one of the prime targets of the blockade was a Russian ship specially fitted to carry ballistic missiles to Cuba and named the Poltavia. The navy was prepared to sink it if necessary to keep its cargo from reaching Castro.

RED ALERT

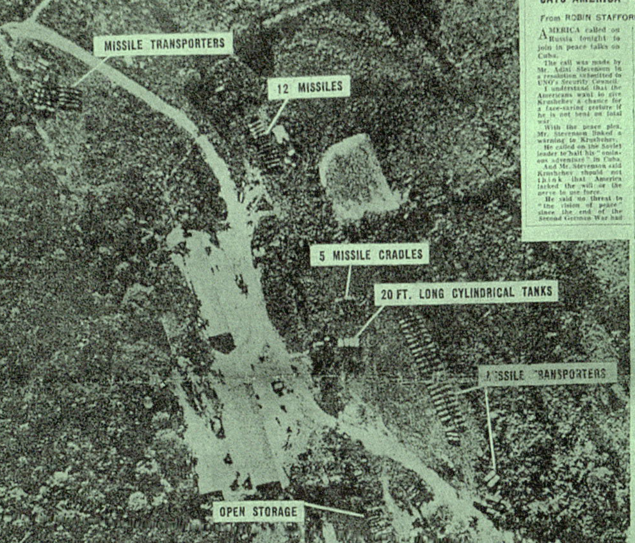

Sky-view of new contours which caused alarm—a missile site. The result: the Cuban blockade

1am: Let's meet and talk

SAYS AMERICA—THEN RUSSIA

From ROBIN STAFFORD: New York, Tuesday

AMERICA called on Russia tonight to join in peace talks on Cuba.

The call was made by Mr. Adlai Stevenson in a resolution submitted to UNO's Security Council.

I understand that the Americans want to give Krushchev a chance for a face-saving gesture if he is not bent on total war.

With the peace plea, Mr. Stevenson linked a warning to Krushchev.

He called on the Soviet leader to "halt his" ominous adventure" in Cuba.

And Mr. Stevenson said Krushchev should not think that America lacked the will or the nerve to use force.

He said no threat to "the vision of peace" since the end of the Second German War had been so profound as the Soviet military build-up in Cuba.

Mr. Stevenson said Cuba had made itself an "accomplice in the Communist enterprise of world dominion."

If the Western hemisphere nations accepted this new phase of aggression, "we would be delinquent in our obligations to world peace."

America wants UNO to demand the dismantling and withdrawal from Cuba of all missiles and other offensive weapons.

To peace

Mr. Stevenson: "There is a road to peace.

"Let this be remembered not as a day when the world came to the edge of nuclear war but as the day when men resolved to let nothing thereafter stop them in their quest for peace."

Russia's Mr. Zorin said America was lying because the picture it painted of a threat by Cuba as completely false.

Then Mr. Zorin asked the Security Council to "insist" that the U.S. call off its blockade.

The resolution tabled by Mr. Zorin also called for negotiations between Russia, the U.S. and Cuba "with the purpose of normalising the situation and removing the threat of war."

4.30 a.m. LATES[T]

16 PEOPLE . . .

9 KILLED . . .

RADIO and TV Turn to Page 17

FLEet street 800[0]

More sky-spy pictures PAGE FIVE

Grosvenor-square 'riot' PAGE TWO

Questions answered PAGE TEN

POCKET CARTOON by OSBERT LANCASTER

CHAPMAN PINCHER

Britain's best-informed defence correspondent reports on the pictures that show Castro's rocket build-up

THE tremendous speed with which the Russians have built up Cuba as a nuclear rocket base has astonished and alarmed U.S. and British defence chiefs.

Already the island is equipped with so many Soviet missiles manned by Red Air Force and Red Army crews that President Kennedy's naval blockade may prove to have been launched too late.

Last night I inspected detailed enlargements of a dozen reconnaissance photographs taken by high-flying U.S. airplanes and released by the American Embassy in London.

I am satisfied they are completely genuine.

... Reconnaissance early in July revealed nothing unusual. But in the next three weeks large numbers of Soviet military men, technicians, and shiploads of equipment arrived.

By the end of August the Russians had completed 16 sites equipped with anti-aircraft guided missiles.

Although concerned at this build-up of defensive weapons, President Kennedy and his advisers felt no action was needed.

But early this month large numbers of Ilyushin 28 bombers, which can carry nuclear bombs with a radius of 1,000 miles, suddenly appeared on several airfields.

An intensive surveillance ...

MINI-CAR CRUSHED —FOUR KILLED

Express Staff Reporter

Broadmoor plot fails

A Broadmoor escape plot has been foiled because a relative of one of the three patients involved tipped off the police.

Boy in a dream woke on roof

The wrong pedal

Barber's rescue

Faultless Tom

Red peace offer

A-blast delayed

Cricket captain names another

Express Staff Reporter

RONNIE BURNET, last amateur captain of Yorkshire cricket club, is named today as co-respondent in a divorce suit.

WEALTHY

Briton goes over to Russians

Wall Street down

Navy men accused

£10,000,000 cars

Holy Loch recall

various examples of art, society, space research and war, and a film on automatic mechanical self-replication. Pete Townshend, later of The Who, who was then an art student, was in the audience and many years later testified to the profound effect that Metzger's lecture had had on his thinking and the direction of his work as a musician in later years.[8] Although Metzger is himself reluctant to take credit for Pete Townshend's signature smashing of a guitar during The Who's performance, he does recall showing one particular slide of the Guitai artist Saburo Murakami in 1956 jumping through a sheet of paper with his arm raised and fist clenched which he likens to the pose often frequently adopted by the musician during performances. At this time the activities of the Gutai group, formed in Osaka in 1954, were not well known in Britain.

Film, Fifth Manifesto and the AA Lecture of 1965

In 1963 Metzger attended the Film Course at the Slade School of Fine Art, London and met Peter Whitehead and Harold Liversidge who, in the summer of 1963 proposed making a film of Metzger demonstrating auto-destructive art. A fifteen minute film was made of Metzger making an acid painting, and staged on the South Bank. It was entitled *Auto-Destructive Art – The Activities of G. Metzger*. Metzger's brother Mendel took photographs of the event which appeared the following year in *Signals* (September 1964) with a reprint of his first four manifestos.[9] On the same page were 'Some Statements' by Jean Tinguely.

Metzger published his fifth manifesto, *On Random Activity in Material. Transforming Works of Art* on 30 July 1964 but perhaps the most significant event of these years was not to come until 24 February 1965 when he gave the Lecture/Demonstration: *Auto-Destructive Art* at the Architectural Association in London, at the invitation of Royston Landau. In this lecture Metzger described a proposal for some monumental, time-based sculptural projects which he considered to be the 'perfect realisation' of auto-destructive art and fulfilled all the criteria set out in the manifesto – they were both public art projects but crucially, they were machine made (human hands only being employed to assist with the construction of the work), and both would auto destruct by the gradual transformation of their material structure caused by the passing of time.

The first monument he proposed was a structure made from steel that would gradually corrode as a result of exposure to the polluted atmosphere. After ten years the work would cease to exist. Metzger made a *Model for Auto-Destructive Monument*, 1960, which was illustrated in the publication of the lecture,[10] and this was re-created for his exhibition at the Kunstraum, München in 1997.

The second proposal was another huge metal structure entitled *Five Screens with*

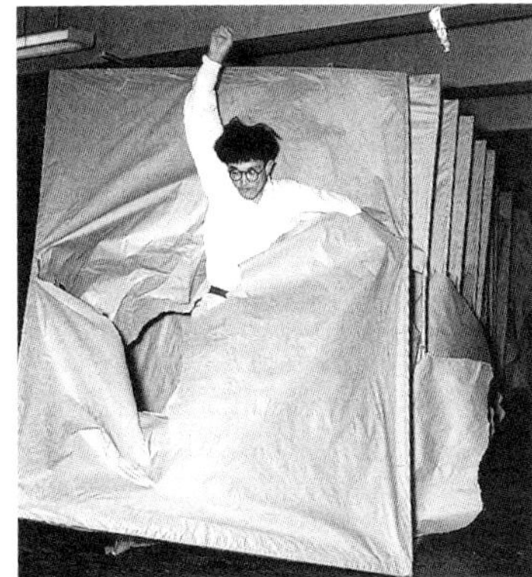

Saburo Murakami,
Many Sheets of Paper,
1959

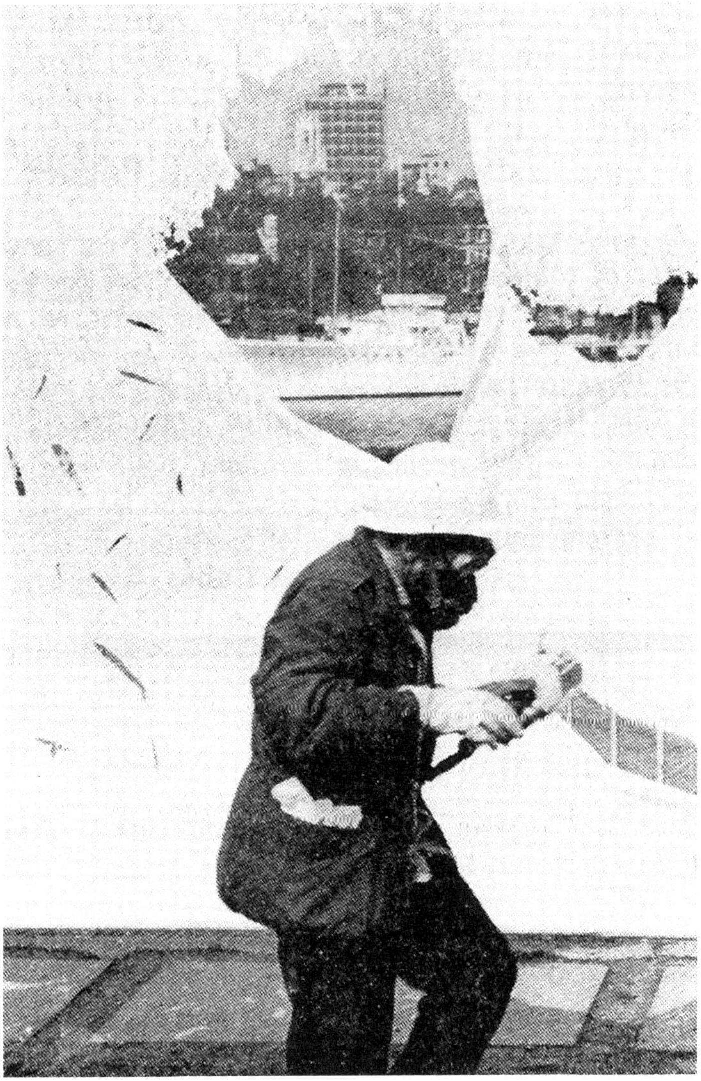

Photograph taken by Mendel Metzger during the filming of Gustav Metzger giving a demonstration of Auto-Destructive Art, 1963

Computer and consisted of stainless steel walls stacked with thousands of smaller uniform parts to be placed between blocks of flats, controlled by a computer. In time, the parts of the structure would be ejected at different speeds, directions and frequencies until after a decade the emptied site would remain.

Metzger was never invited to undertake either of these ambitious projects although he was to continue working on *Five Screens With Computer*, his biggest project, until 1972, utilising models and computer graphics, and through consulting with scientists and historians of science. To date the best example of auto-destructive art remains his acid-nylon paintings. However, as these were made by hand, he considers that these do not perfectly reflect the ideal set out in the manifesto.

The AA lecture was published in June 1965 and republished in October and has remained Metzger's key text on the subject of auto-destructive art and the basis for much of his subsequent work.

DIAS, September 1966

Through all of Metzger's artistic career, he is perhaps best known for initiating one event, The Destruction in Art Symposium – DIAS which took place in London throughout September 1966. This month-long event drew an international gathering of somewhere in the region of a hundred artists from different disciplines who were unified in exploring the concept of the potential for creativity in destruction through various Happenings, lectures, poetry readings and performances.[11] As the DIAS press release states, 'The main objective of DIAS was to focus attention on the element of destruction in Happenings and other art forms, and to relate this to destruction in society'. Participants included Wolf Vostell, Ivor Davies, Hermann Nitsch, Yoko Ono and John Latham.

A special 'Auto Destructive' issue of the journal *Art and Artists* came out the month before DIAS in anticipation of the event and included articles on and by many of the artists who were to participate.[12]

As secretary and main organiser of the event, Metzger gave a keynote lecture but did not himself partipate, his main reason being that he felt that the work he was doing was quite different for it was specifically concerned with 'auto-destruction', not destruction per se. In the months leading up to the event, letters written by Metzger (on specially printed DIAS letterhead) to Ivor Davies who was a particularly active member of the organising committee, reveal a lot about the tremendous pace at which the Symposium took shape and the incredible response from artists all over the world as news of the event quickly spread. One letter, dated 18 August read 'We are getting 30–40 communications a week now... Three artists from Vienna are coming. They make fantastic Material Aktionen.

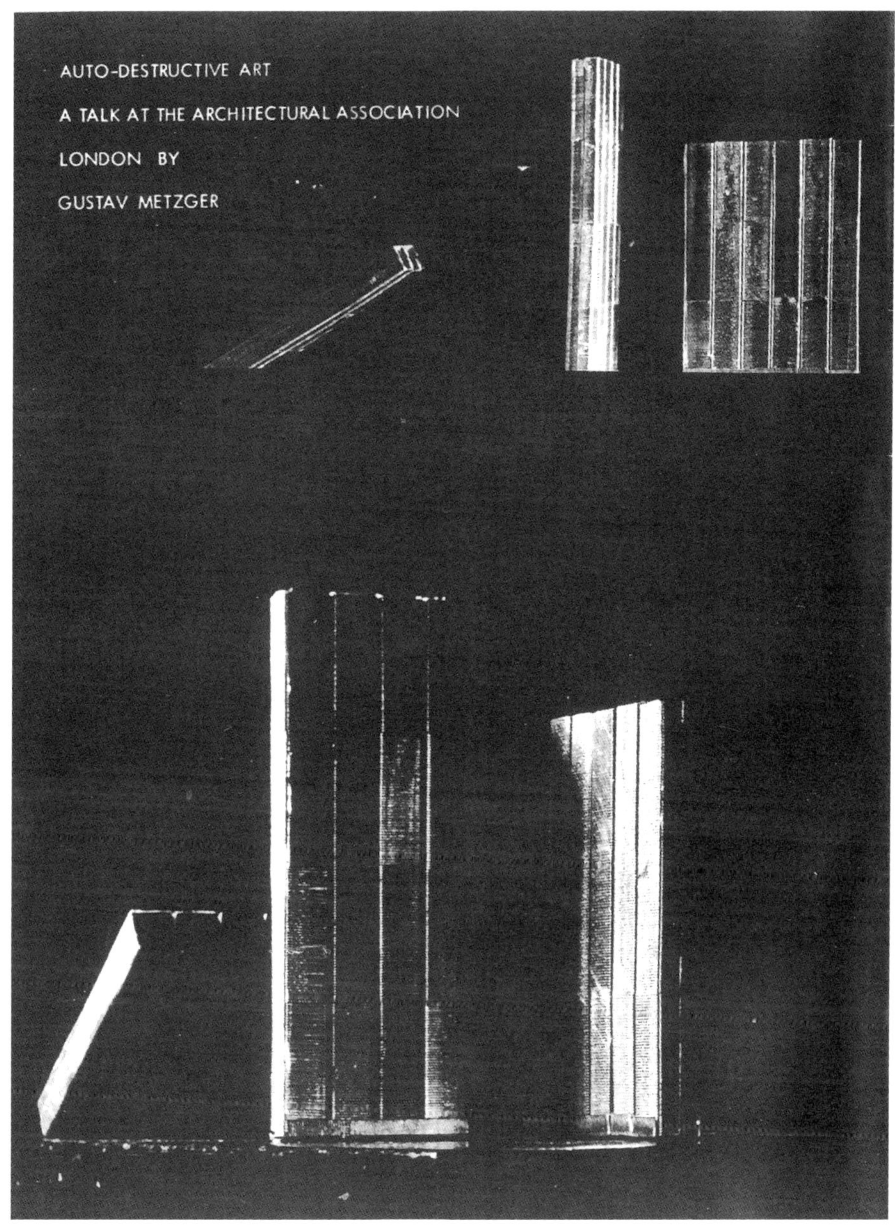

Model for Auto-Destructive Monument, 1960 illustrated in the publication of a talk given at the Architectural Association in 1965

Sensational photos have arrived for the show'.[13] This was to be the first time the Viennese Actionists performed outside of their own country. Metzger has since been credited as an important figure in promoting their activities.

As Kristine Stiles, who has written extensively on the subject of DIAS has commented: 'A list of those who participated in the organising committee of DIAS alone, suggests how this event marked a significant moment in the history of international exchange amongst artists and poets associated with the Left counter-culture concerned with destruction with art and society at this time'.[14] Metzger has since acknowledged that part of the success of DIAS was due to its timing, coming as it did in the midst of the Vietnam War.

The event was covered widely by the national and international press and, most memorably in the group photograph shown in *Life* magazine and *Art and Artists*. However, it was some of the controversy associated with the the event which seemed to create the largest impression, as exemplified in Arthur Moyse's article which appeared in *Freedom* just a few days after he witnessed Hermann Nitsch's action on 16 September, which he condemns as a 'vile and obscene act'.[15] Nitsch's action resulted in Metzger, together with John Sharkey, as members of the organising committee, being charged with 'unlawfully causing to be shown and presented an indecent exhibition contrary to Common Law.' At the court trial Metzger was fined £100 and John Sharkey was conditionally discharged.

In the *DIAS Preliminary Report*, published on February 1967, Metzger gives his own account of the events of the Symposium. The first page of the report, which was designed by Metzger, contains a hand-written statement sent by Ad Reinhardt who, unable to attend DIAS, wanted to make a contribution. Metzger kept the spirit of DIAS active with the subsequent publication of *DIAS-Information* sheets, of which five in all were issued up to March 1968.

Liquid Crystal Light Projections 1965–98

It was in February 1963 during a Lecture/Demonstration given for the Bartlett Society, at the University of London, that Metzger made his first light projections in which nylon, stretched on a slide frame, was seen to disintegrate after the application of hydrochloric acid.

On 7 September in 1965 Metzger showed his light projection *Notes on the Chemical Revolution in Art* at a fundraising gala for the ICA, organised by Mark Boyle, at the Theatre Royal in Stratford, London. It was a rear projection with three adapted stage projectors, aided by assistants. This was the first large-scale 'light-show' to be seen in England. In a recent interview with Andrew Wilson, Metzger recalled how this display was greeted by stunned silence from the audience,

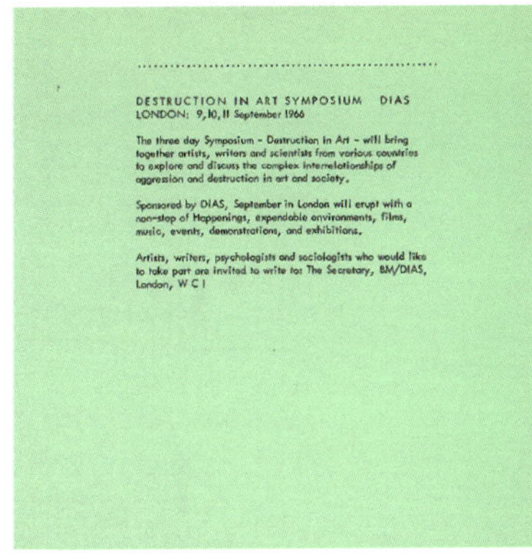

DESTRUCTION IN ART SYMPOSIUM DIAS
LONDON: 9,10,11 September 1966

The three day Symposium – Destruction in Art – will bring together artists, writers and scientists from various countries to explore and discuss the complex interrelationships of aggression and destruction in art and society.

Sponsored by DIAS, September in London will erupt with a non-stop of Happenings, expendable environments, films, music, events, demonstrations, and exhibitions.

Artists, writers, psychologists and sociologists who would like to take part are invited to write to: The Secretary, BM/DIAS, London, W C I

Flyer promoting DIAS,
September 1966

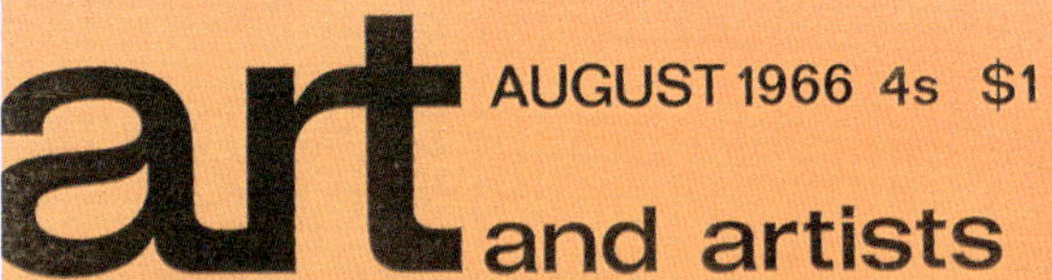

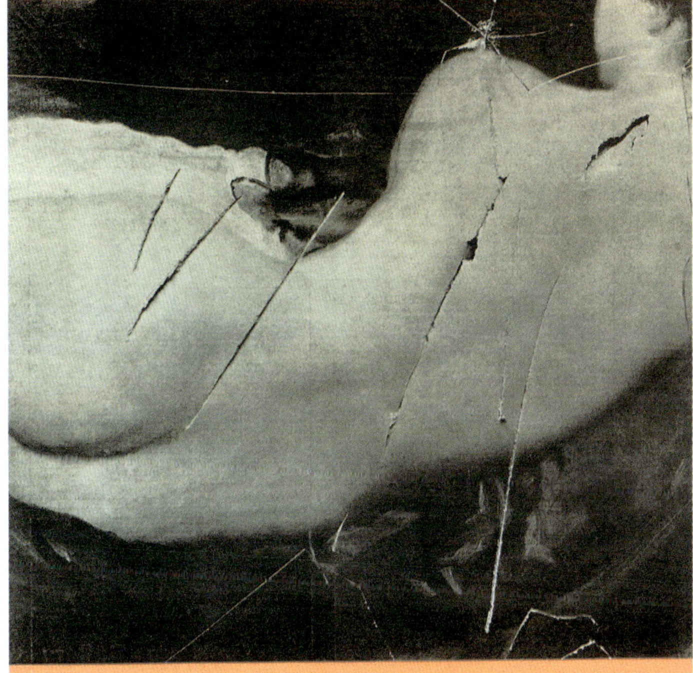

Front cover of
'Auto-Destructive'
issue of *Art and Artists*,
August 1966

DIAS

DESTRUCTION IN ART SYMPOSIUM

London. 8th 9th 10th Sept. 1966
11th.

Ivor Davies
44 Clive Place
Penarth

Communications to : BM/DIAS
London WC I

Telegraphic address : BM/DIAS
c/o Monomark
London

29.7.1966.

Dear Ivor,

Just to confirm our Committee meeting - next Thursday, Hotel Sharuna, Gt. Russell Street, W.C.1. MUS.5922/3/4. At 7.30, meal followed by meeting in lounge.

I think Symposium venue now solved.
We have Cochrane cleared 100% for Sunday only. Price about 25£.
We can have marvellous 19th.C hall, with delicate cast-iron work near Covent Garden, all day Friday and Saturday, total for 2 days, 25£. Seats up to 200 people. Also has full cafe and restaurant facilities downstairs. This is Africa Centre, Hinsley House, King Street, W.C.2. Try to see this before meeting.

Things are hotting up. 3cables from New York yesterday. Al Hansen is setting up a press conference, and Belgian artist there coming to London in September wants to arrange destructive event with us.

Hope your work and luggage arrived safely.

Lookforward to see you. If you will be in London much of Thursday, write to me at hpme address, and we can meet via John Sharkey in day time perhaps.

Yours,
Gustav

Letter to Ivor Davies, dated 29 July 1966

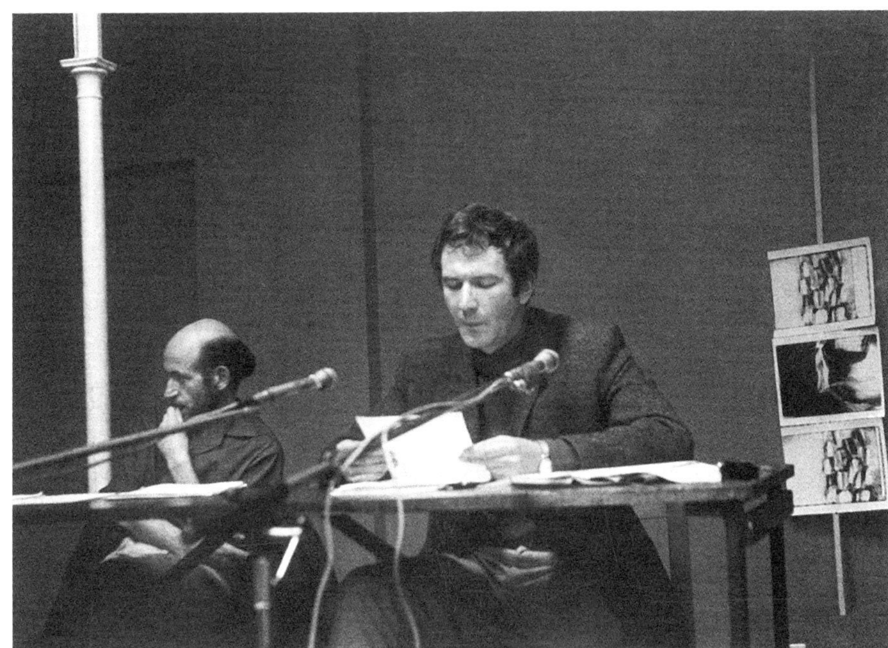

Ivor Davies and Gustav Metzger at DIAS, 9 September, 1966. Photo: Hanns Sohm, courtesty of the Sohm Archive, Stuttgart

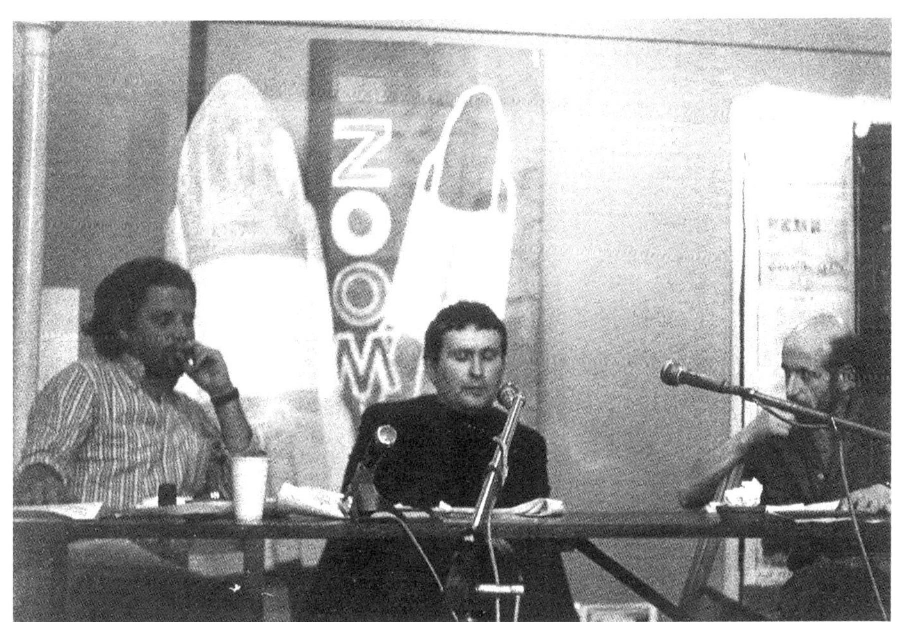

Hermann Nitsch presenting his text at DIAS . Photo: Hanns Sohm, courtesty of the Sohm Archive, Stuttgart

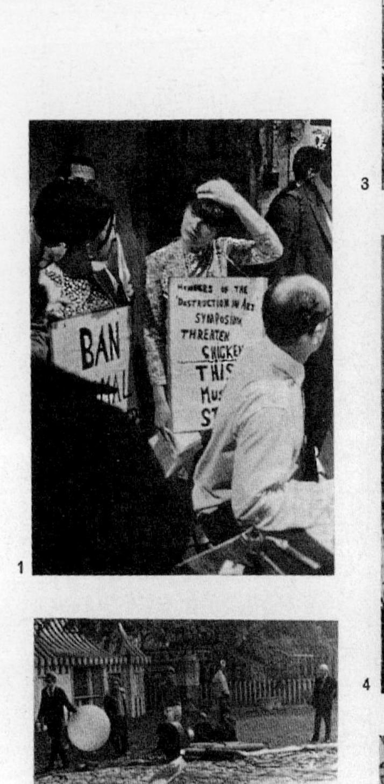

1

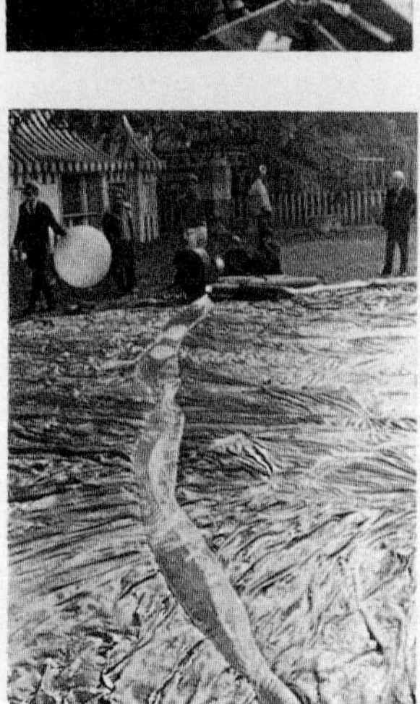

2

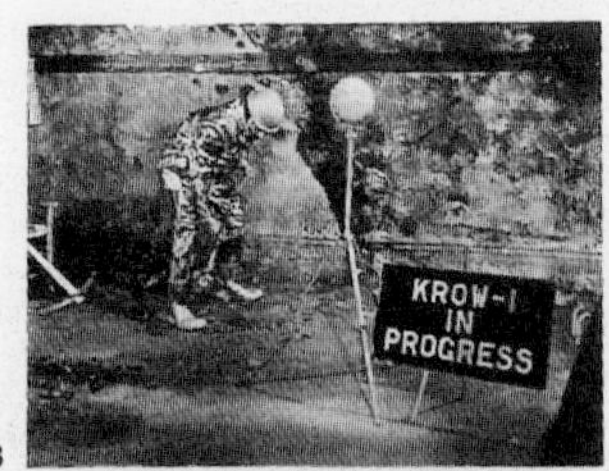

3

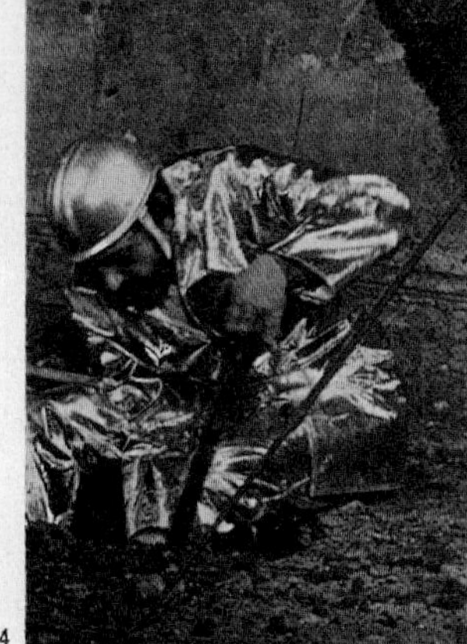

4

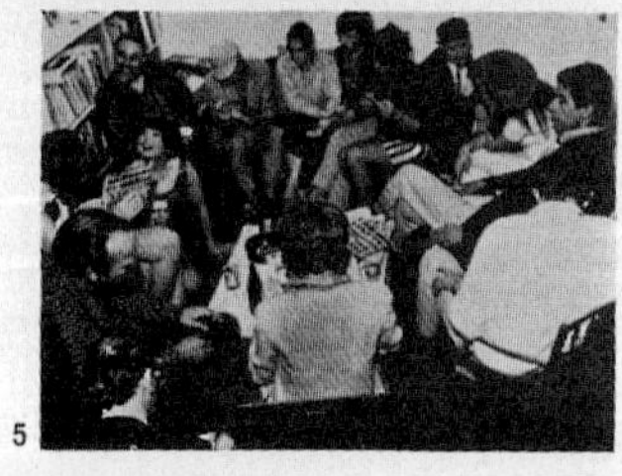

5

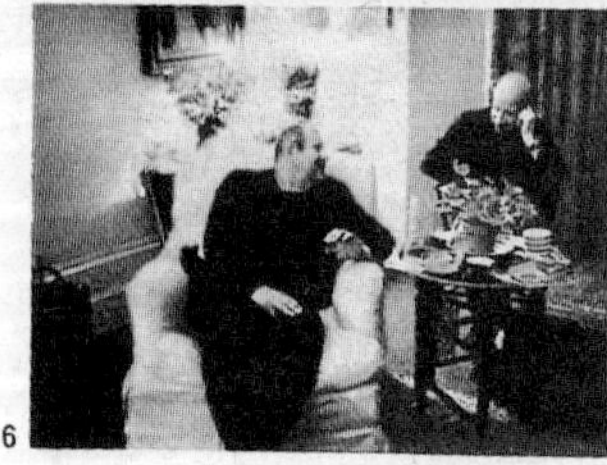

6

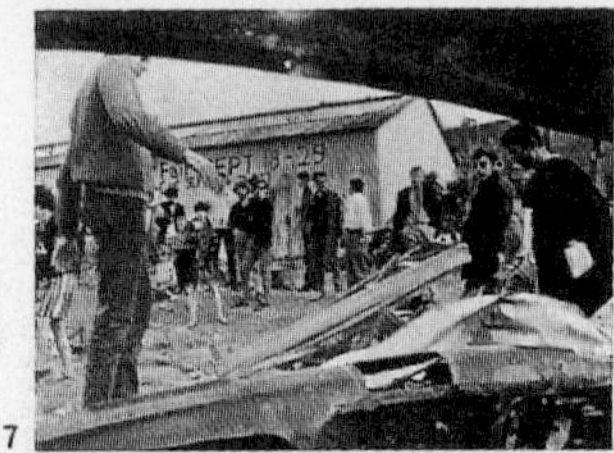

7

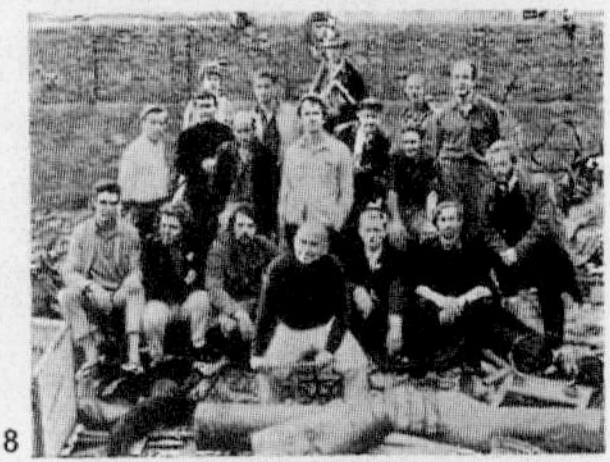

8

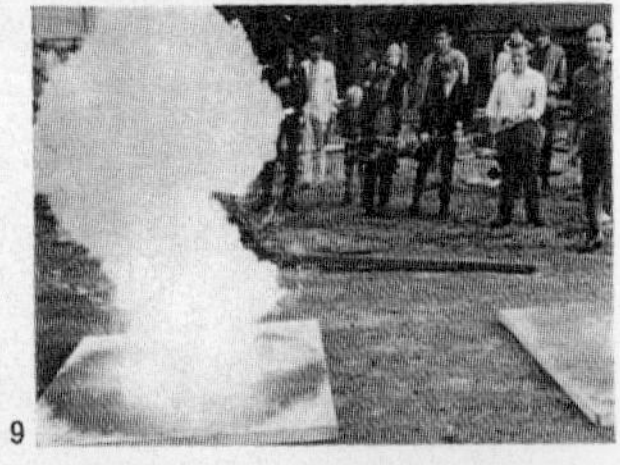

9

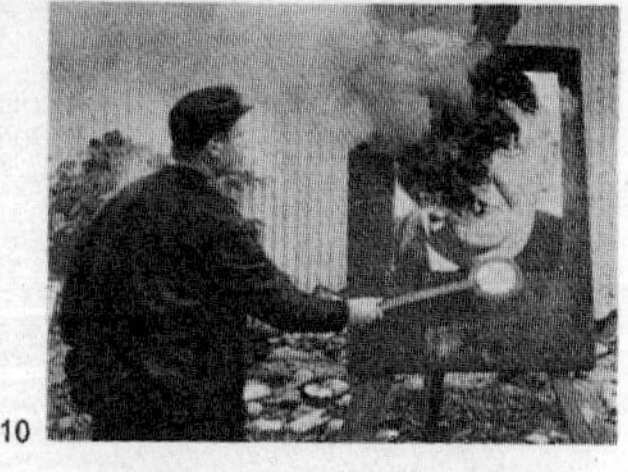

10

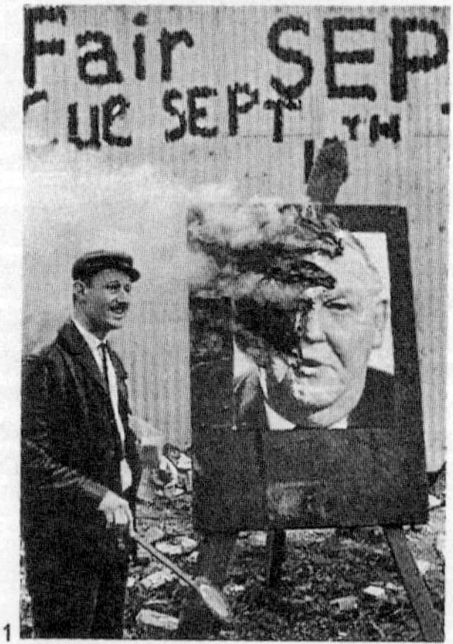

11

Coverage of DIAS in *Art and Artists*, October 1966, including photographs of the event taken by John Prosser

DIAS

Destruction In Art

The international Symposium of Destruction in Art was held in London during the week beginning the 9th of September. It was attended by many visitors from Europe and America, and events, discussions and lectures took place in various parts of the city. These photographs were taken by John Prosser.

1 Protestors at Better Books, Charing Cross Road

2 Biff Stevens: 'Balloon' Happening, Battersea Park

3 Robin Page: 'Krow-1' at Better Books basement

4 Robin Page in the Hole

5 'Art and Artists' party for DIAS

6 Wolf Vostell and Gustav Metzger at the party

7 An event in a playground, Acklam Road

8 The DIAS Group

9 A picture-burning by Pro Diaz

10 & 11 Werner Schreib: 'Death of Lucullus'

12 Symposium in progress at the Africa Centre

13 John Sharkey and Yoko Ono at the Symposium

14 Robin Page, Jasia Reichardt and Hans Sohm at the Symposium

15 Gustav Metzger, Wolf Vostell, Al Hansen and Hidalgo at the Symposium

16 Ivor Davies at the Symposium

17 Fred Hunter in the 'Paper' Happening, Conway Hall

18 Otto Mühl and Günter Brus: 'Breathing' event, Conway Hall

19 Ralph Ortiz: 'Paper' Happening, Conway Hall

20 Yoko Ono on stage, Conway Hall

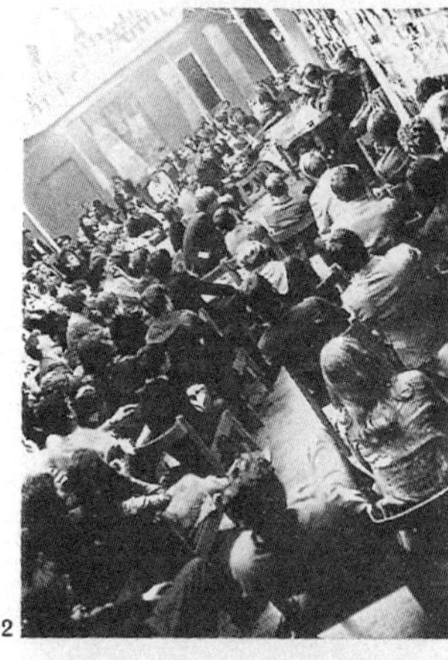

12

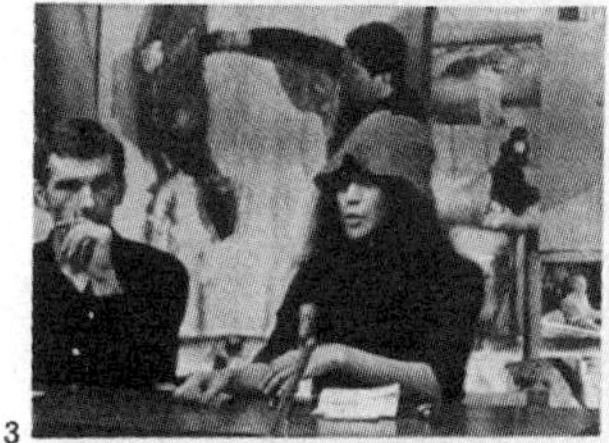

13

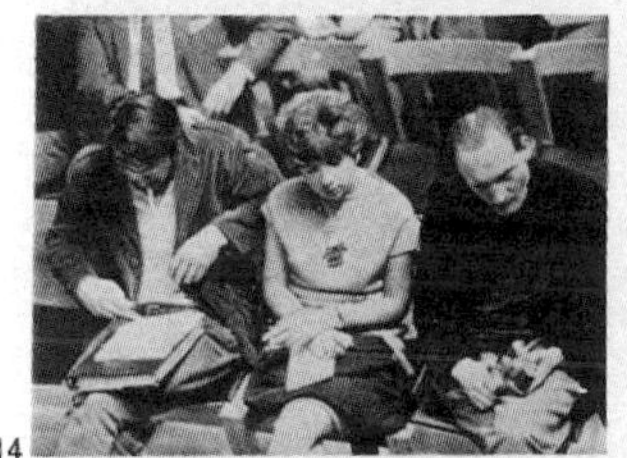

14

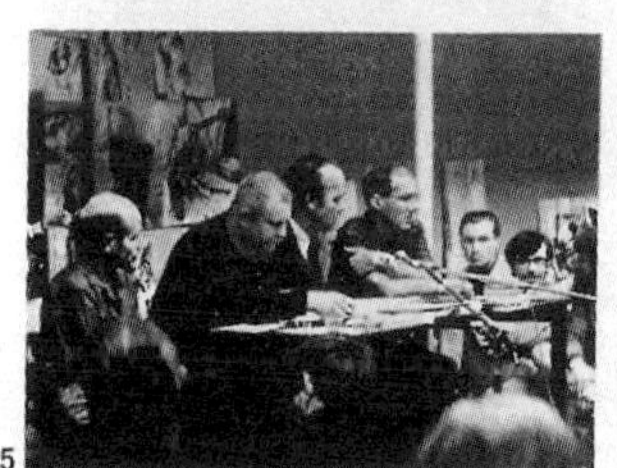

15

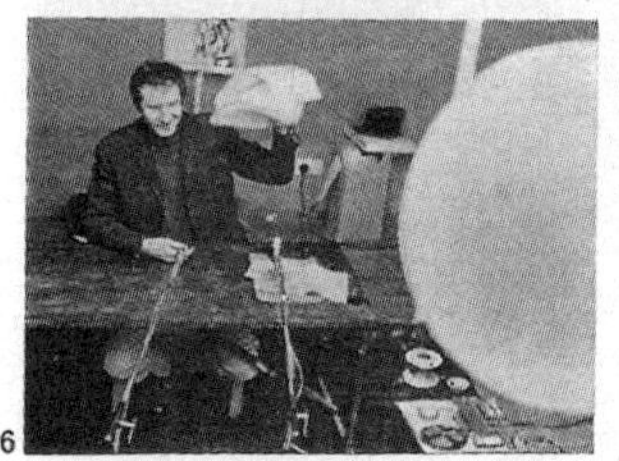

16

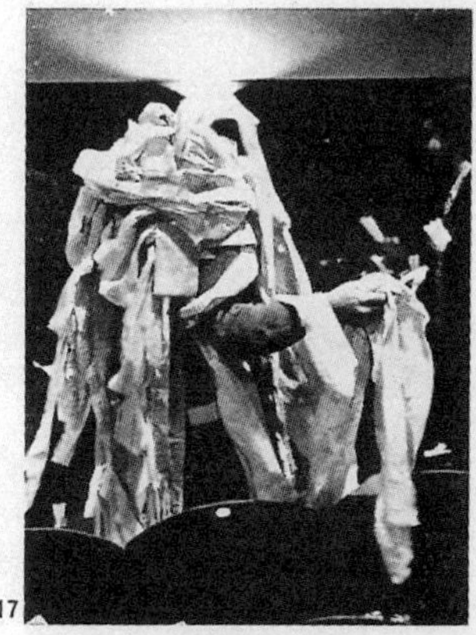

17

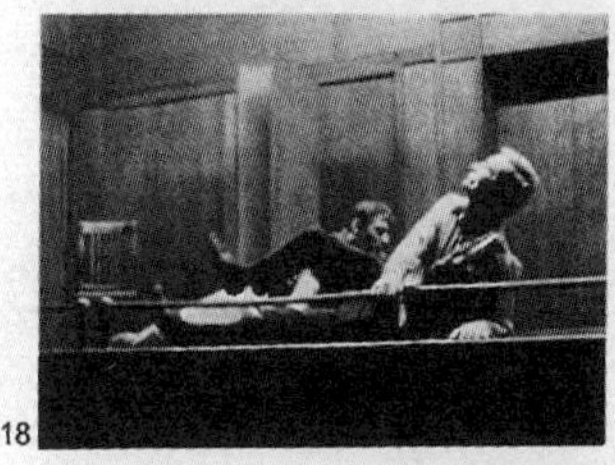

18

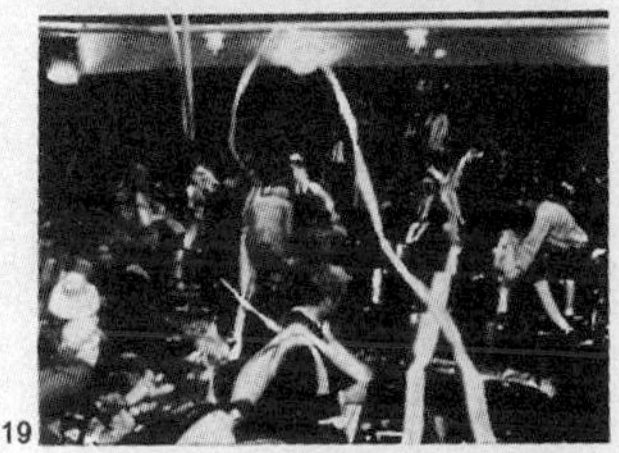

19

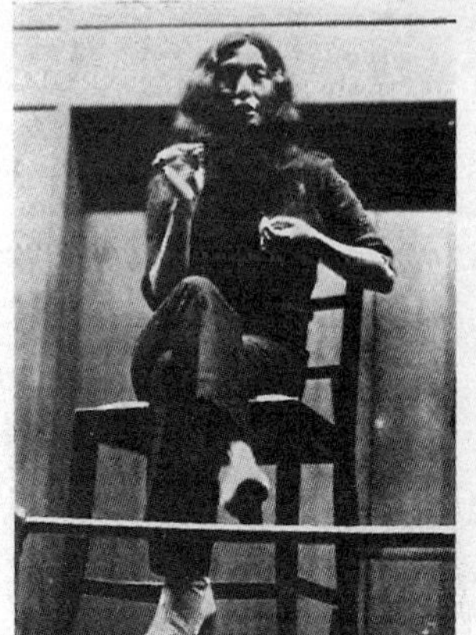

20

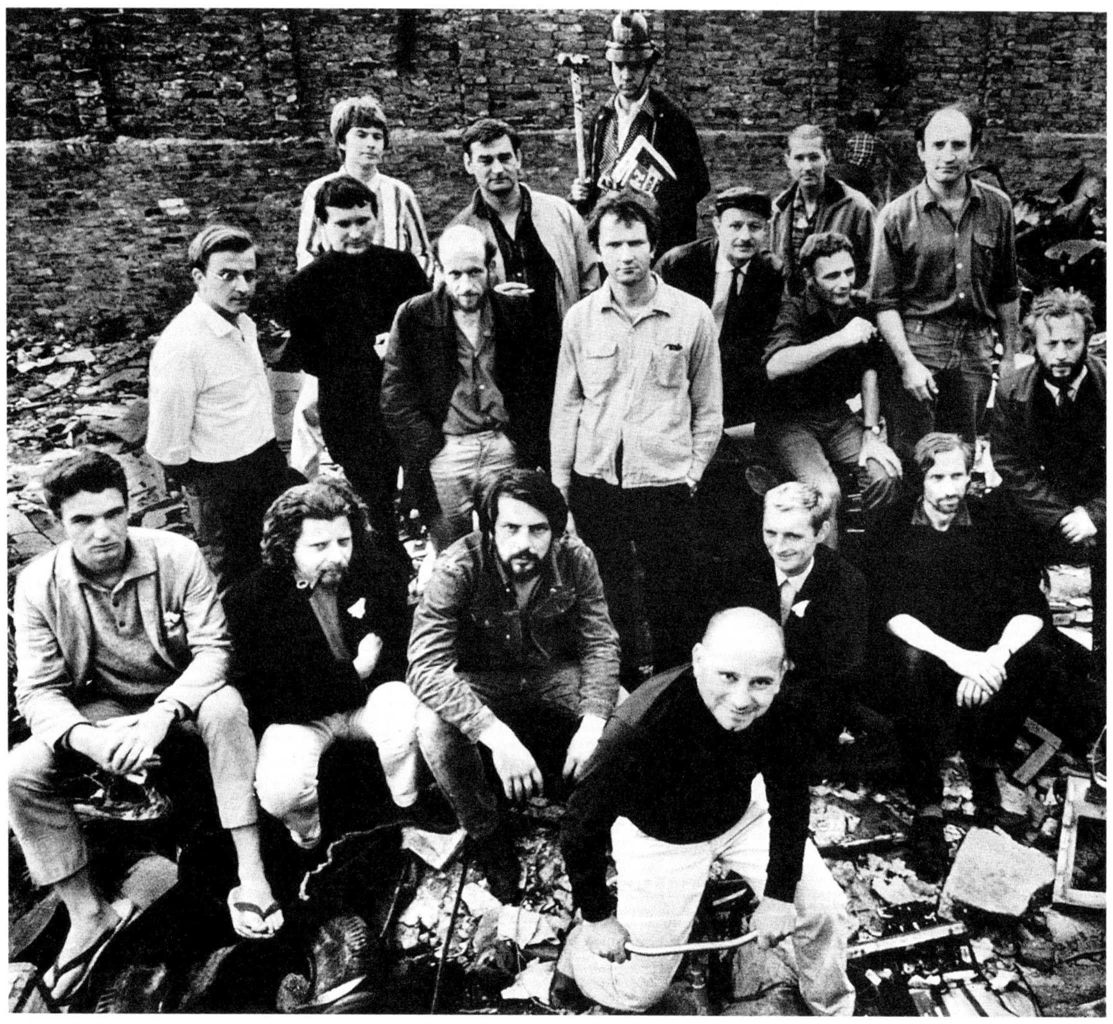

Group photograph of members of DIAS which appeared in *Life* magazine, February, 1967.
Photo: Tom Picton

Arthur Moyse's article on DIAS for *Freedom*, London, September 1966

MANIFESTO OF THE DEAD

WITHIN EVERY SOCIETY there are those who advance their political, social or aesthetic theories only to the limitations that the tolerance of their particular society will allow them. One accepts this for all of us, with but a few minor exceptions, compromise in the living of our daily lives with those forces we profess to hate or reject. But what cannot be condoned are those who ally themselves with the very creatures that they are in conflict with.

When certain CND officials openly conferred with major police officials on the policing of their meeting we despised them for what we held to be their final act of public impotence. When trade union officials take their seats on government and managerial boards we no longer trust them for we know that they are now the creatures of divided loyalties, and when a group of men and women under the umbrella title of ART scream death and destruction as an aesthetic theory yet only operate within the sterile area of the art magazine, the gossip column of the daily press and the middle-class culture flop house in Dover Street, then we feel that we are justified in dismissing this as another giggle for the Town as banal and pretentious as a Billy Graham meeting. Al Hanson who was billed to perform in a bomb crater in Carnaby Street has written that THE FUTUROS ADMIRES WAR, EXPLOSIONS, PUNCHES ON THE NOSE . . . THERE IS A CONTEMPORARY ARTIST, LATHAN, WHO BURNS AND MESSES UP BOOKS . . . DOES THE CARPENTER SAWING UP THE NEAT NEW LENGTHS OF WOOD REALIZE HOW DELICIOUS IT IS TO BE RAPING AND MAIMING? THE ART OF A DESTRUCTIVE ACT IS ALWAYS FRESH.

Yet they were but idle words that drifted ceilingwise for three days in the Victorian hall of the Africa Centre and while the bearded lads and jerseyed lassies listened to the bilingual polemics from the platform death, gay and indifferent, played out their farce in South Africa where Dimitri Tsafendas, without a single paid line in *Art and Artists*, successfully tried out the ancient art form on the body of Dr. Verwoerd. This is the tragedy of all these bright little get-togethers that no one, least of all the authorities, trouble to take them seriously. It has been said, and with complete justice, that Laurel and Hardy did the Ortiz piano-smashing act with greater professional skill and more humour—for if anything could be held to damn this monotonous smashing of commercial rejects it is that after the second showing it is no longer funny ha-ha. If the end product that you offer is trivial then it must follow that the means must be all-important and as with all popular culture movements it is the personalities of the performers, no matter how meagre their talents, that become the focal point for the interest of the audience. As with all publicity movements the DIAS event produced its rash of prima donnas led by the German Wolf Vostell who refused to exhibit his *de-collages* in the basement of Better Books because, so the Town whispers, he could not have a white wall or because of the low standard of the other work. Whatever the reason, true or false, it is of little import in relation to this work of such little import.

With Vostell and the *hand/and/eye* squad gone we were left with Gustav Metzger and the spoken word. Metzger has played an odd role in this event. A tiny, bald and gently spoken man, born one feels out of his era, he has long been schooled and hardened in the politics of the militant left and he has handled the whole of the DIAS affair, from its conception to its death, with a political brilliance and brutality. It has been held that he has used Wolf Vostell's book *Happenings* as a bible and a social register and deliberately excluded men like Nuttall and Keen because they were not part of the Vostell sacred text.

True, false or indifferent, one can only raise a tired eyebrow at a destruction-in-art event that does not include work by Bruce Lacey—but committees are committees and editors are editors. During the course of the polemic Metzger acted out his role of policeman with, it is claimed, threats to eject any unfortunate who should dare to interrupt while in his MI5 act he would rise from the body of the hall and read out the *crime sheet* of any known offbeat that chose to speak or protest. When I protested at the enlarged photograph of a skinned and crucified lamb I had to sit in silence for at least a minute while Metzger, unasked, rose from behind me and read out my associations and my attitude towards the arts. I was then allowed to speak. Yet my public protest was no idle one for while Nitsch is at liberty to pose his friends in the guise of freshly castrated subjects, complete with imitation blood, I would hold that it is a vile and obscene act, in the true meaning of these words, to crucify the skinned body of an animal to amuse an audience and whether *'the animal was dead when used'* does not lessen the evil of this loathsome act. When, in America, Ay-O guillotined a chicken and the unfortunate creature staggered around bleeding to death this was held to be a gay little giggle. Much was made at this symposium that God is dead so by that very statement life is sacred.

Man is the only creature who can conceive the awfulness of death so that if these stupid people within the Africa Centre wish to kill or sup at second hand the bestiality of death then let them kill each other and not while away a hot summer afternoon by applauding those who have chosen to persecute the innocent in the name of science, religion, politics or even ART.

ARTHUR MOYSE.

DIAS
DESTRUCTION IN ART SYMPOSIUM — PRELIMINARY REPORT
London. 9,10,11, September, 1966.

The cataclysmic increase in world destructive potential since 1945, is inextricably linked with the most disturbing tendencies in modern art, and the proliferation of programmes of research into aggression and destruction

PROGRAM FOR PROGRAM-PAINTING

1. THE RE-DESTRUCTION OF THE VERTICAL STRIPE AND HORIZONTAL BAND IN ART.
2. THE RE-DISSOLUTION OF LINE AND EDGE, COLOR AND CONTRAST IN ART.
3. THE RE-OBLITERATION OF TEXTURE AND BRUSHWORK IN ART.
4. THE RE-ABROGATION OF ASYMMETRIC COMPOSITION IN ART.
5. THE RE-ANNIHILATION OF THE SCU ND SMEAR IN ART.
6. THE RE-DEMOLITION OF SHAPE, FI AND SIGN IN ART.
7. THE RE-NEGATION OF STYLIZATION, SPONTANEITY IN ART.
8. THE RE-NULLIFICATION OF SUBJECT D REACTION IN ART.
9. THE RE-EXTERMINATION OF NEO-EX ALISM AND NEO-POP IN ART.
10. THE RE-DEVASTATION OF MEANING, ITY AND RUSTICITY IN ART.

AD REINHARDT, 1966, NEW YORK

THE GUARDIAN

London — Friday September 9, 1966

Art that is ripe for destruction

The Destruction-in-Art boys are among us and we shall ignore them, as they put it, only at our peril. They are from 10 countries and have assembled in London for a three-day symposium starting today. They will exhibit photographs of men sitting in the dripping blood of eviscerated animals, which is said to be art; they have bashed a hole in the basement floor of a London bookshop and struck water, which is said to be art; they are bickering over whose works shall be exhibited, and with them this also is said to be an art. Some of them would like to stamp on frogs or crucify a lamb. They have smashed up a piano, though Laurel and Hardy used to do it better.

Now, why shouldn't an artist affront us to make us see what he wants us to see? If he shows us men sitting under a bleeding sheep it may only be to remind us that we usually eat the sheep without thinking that it died, which is fair enough. And the destroyers have at least a case when they argue, as they seem to argue, that men are violent and that this violence may be diverted: better that canvases should be ripped, or chickens decapitated, than that a single man should be hurt. But pictures of women bundled up in transparent sacks, or of men smeared with blood and muck, whatever the artistic purpose, are more likely to degrade than to exalt. Violence makes violence.

The destroyers-in-art include writers who obliterate words, burn books, and cut odd words out of dictionaries and paste them up haywire. They tear books apart and shuffle the pages so that the narrative now reads surprisingly (which is art). Words are displaced and lines transposed in a new and meaningful way. Some newspapers, it seems, especially in their hurried first editions, have long possessed a natural aptitude for the new and the meaningful. That's art. Or is it? More often it is error. Just as destruction-in-art is mainly perverse, ugly, and anti-social.

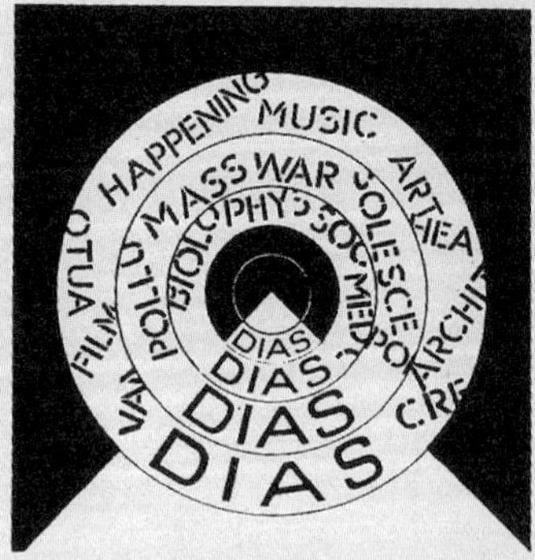

Cover of DIAS *Preliminary Report*, featuring Ad Reinhardt's text, February 1967

PAPA WHAT DID YOU DO WHEN THE NAZIS BUILT THE CONCENTRATION CAMPS MY DEAR THEY NEVER TOLD US ANYTHING

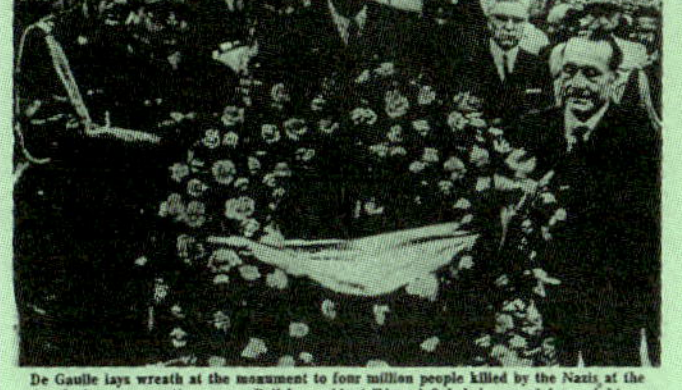

De Gaulle lays wreath at the monument to four million people killed by the Nazis at the Auschwitz concentration camp. Polish president Edward Ochab is second from right

US planning 'death ray' weapon

FROM OUR OWN CORRESPONDENT

NEW YORK, SEPT. 5

The United States Atomic Energy Commission is pressing research towards a neutron bomb —an enhanced radiation weapon crudely described as a sort of death ray. In a joint statement the A.E.C. and the Defence Department said:

"Such a device would be very 'clean'. The term 'very clean' would mean a device in which only a small amount of the energy released would come from fission The blast effect would be very small, but the radiation effect from neutrons would be predominant The A.E.C. is also conducting research on pure fusion weapons."

The statement said:—

The United States has a stockpile of tens of thousands of individual nuclear weapons, ranging in power from less than a kiloton (the equivalent of 1,000 tons of T.N.T.) to several megatons (millions of tons of T.N.T.).

They include artillery-fired projectiles, atomic demolition munitions, anti-submarine rockets and torpedoes, depth charges, strategic and tactical missiles, and bombs.

Chinese tests

Overall, the departments believe the United States maintains a nuclear weapons superiority over the Soviet Union.

"The Chinese nuclear tests to date", the statement observes, "indicate a rational, well organized nuclear weapons development programme....

"A launch of an intercontinental ballistic missile test vehicle by China this year would be necessary if they are to meet the most rapid deployment schedules considered possible. . . . There will be a period of testing and missile improvement.

"If the Chinese then achieve a first operational I.C.B.M. capability in the 1970-1972 period, it is possible they will have a significant deployment in the mid-1970s."

292 SCIENCE FOR ALL.

indiscriminate voracity for vegetable substances. In the Old World, if there is one species (amongst several) which may be termed *par excellence* "the

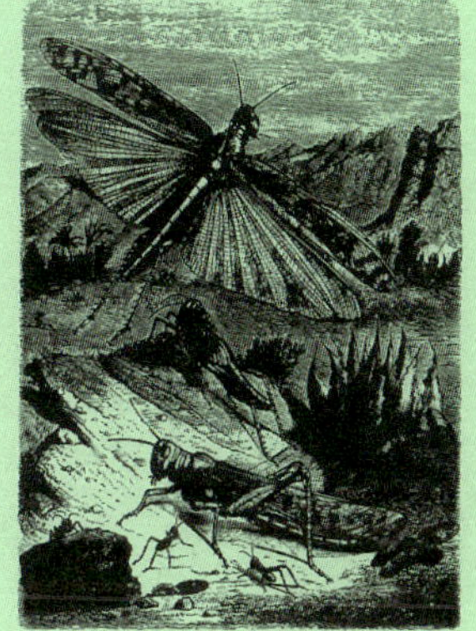

FIG. 7.—METAMORPHOSIS OF THE LOCUST (*Acrydium peregrinum*).

locust," it is *Pachytylus migratorius*. In North America, on the other hand, the locust is *Caloptenus spretus*, the Rocky Mountain locust.

If we trace the history of a band of the latter, we will be able to form some idea of how locusts commit such havoc amongst vegetation. After they are hatched, the young locusts begin to show their social or gregarious proclivities by congregating together in warm and sunny spots, feeding upon such plants as are most attractive to them. As they increase in size they require more food, and

LOCUSTS AND GRASSHOPPERS. 293

by their great numbers soon clear the ground of vegetation. Till after the first moult (that is, the first true moult, not the casting of the pellicle that enveloped them when first hatched) they, however, do not commence to migrate. After that, having eaten up all the food in their vicinity, they are forced to set out on their travels in search of more food. They march, often in a swarm a mile wide, during the warmer hours of the day, clearing out everything eatable in their path. When they come to woods they first of all clear out the brushwood, and eat the dead leaves and bark. "A few succeed in climbing up into the rougher-barked trees, where they feed upon the foliage, and it is amusing to see with what avidity the famished individuals below scramble for any fallen leaf that the more fortunate mounted ones may chance to sever." They continue to increase in destructiveness till after the third moult, after which they begin to decrease in numbers, from starvation, disease, and the attack of enemies. Comparatively few attain the perfect or winged condition, and then return, so far as they are able, to the places where they were hatched, not many miles distant, and do comparatively little damage.

In many respects, the life of the Old World locusts, especially the migratory locust (*Pachytylus migratorius*) is similar to the one just sketched. Like the Rocky Mountain locust, the migratory locust does not commence to migrate till after the first moult, and not to any great extent till after the second. Their time of marching is generally the morning and evening, and they also devour (as they did in the summer of 1880 in Southern Russia) almost every green thing, leaving a wilderness behind them. When they attain the winged condition they do not cease from the work of destruction, and occasionally fly in immense swarms and to great distances. Multitudes of one kind of locust, *Acrydium peregrinum* (Fig. 7), perhaps the species mentioned in the tenth chapter of Exodus, were once seen during a storm in the Atlantic 1,200 miles from land, and great swarms of the same species interrupted the march of a French army in Algeria. (Fig. 3). As a rule, however, it is supposed that they do not wander far from the districts in which they were hatched.

In the northern half of Europe (including Britain) locusts of several kinds occasionally appear, but generally only in small numbers, and without doing any mischief. South, however, of a line drawn from Spain, through the south of France, Switzerland, Roumania, South Russia, and South Siberia, to the north of China, they have again and again wrought dire havoc. A few of the more noted devastations may be mentioned. These devastations—where every plant is devoured—entail of course the starvation of the men and beasts whose food supply has been thus taken from them. But the mischief does not cease with that. Pestilence usually follows, and is produced or aggravated by the effluvia from the decaying bodies of the dead locusts, especially when, as has been frequently the case, the insects have been blown into the sea, and afterwards cast up on the shore by the waves. On one occasion (about the end of last century) so many perished in the sea on part of the African coast that a bank three or four feet high, and about fifty miles long, was formed on the shore by their dead bodies, and the stench of them was carried 150 miles by the wind. In another part of Africa, early in the Christian era, one plague of locusts is said to have caused the death of 800,000 persons; and in 591 nearly as bad a plague occurred in Italy. Again, in 1478, more than 30,000 persons perished in the Venetian territories from famine caused by locusts. Since that time there have been, unfortunately, too many records of locust-plagues, from which it would seem that the old stories are by no means exaggerated. In more than one account, and these comparatively recent, the swarms are described as so dense as to have actually eclipsed the sun, and this not for a few minutes, but for hours at a time, so that when the prophet Joel says that before them "the sun and moon shall be dark, and the stars withdraw their shining," he was speaking literally, and not metaphorically.

There have been, naturally, many attempts made either to prevent or to arrest the plagues of locusts, and in the United States of America the Government some years ago appointed an Entomological Commission to investigate and report on the best means of accomplishing these very desirable objects. As prevention is better than cure, it is evident that steps taken to destroy the eggs or newly-hatched insects will prove most efficacious, a plan which was long (and may still be) in use in the south of France. In other places, to destroy the half or full grown insects, trenches are dug in the ground, into which they are driven, and then destroyed by being covered with earth.

From a very remote antiquity locusts have formed an article of food, not only in Africa and Asia, but even in ancient times in Europe. Sometimes they are smoked or salted, at others they are fried or

Photo. Sunday Times, 10. 9. 1967 Above. The Times, 6. 9. 1967.

Text. "Science for All". Edited by Robert Brown, London, 1893.

DIAS INFORMATION 4. September 1967.

From: BM/DIAS, London, W. C. 1.

DIAS Information 4,
September 1967

an effect which greatly pleased organiser Boyle and other participants.[16]

Metzger's continued work with slide projections and further reading about science and technology and the natural world led him to his first experiments with the use of liquid crystals in projections during a Lecture/Demonstration, *The Chemical Revolution in Art*, for the Society of Arts at Cambridge University, in October 1965. He has since acknowledged the development of *Liquid Crystal Projections* as being his clearest example of auto creative art.

The principle of the liquid crystal technique is as follows: thin glass slides containing liquid crystal are heated and inserted into projectors with a polarized filter placed over the lens. The resulting image is projected on to a screen. As the crystals cool, they change from black at the hottest stage to grey, then gradually become awash with every colour from the spectrum – from green to yellow, purple, red, blue and pink – transforming into endless and irrepeatable combinations.

These projects appear to embody the words defined in his manifesto, an 'art of change, growth, movement' which is constantly renewable, never the same twice. An art of beauty is created by applying the techniques of science and mechanical intervention to the material.

In January 1966, Metzger exhibited the first street display of the liquid crystals phenomena in a window display, *Art of Liquid Crystals* at Better Books in London. The press viewing was on 6 January. He described the technique in a press release titled *Art of Liquid Crystals*, and he became widely established as the first artist to work with this phenomena. On the 8 January, again at Better Books, Metzger showed more light projections in *An Evening of Auto-Destructive and Auto-Creative Art* in which Frank Popper participated.

From 29 March to 16 April, Metzger had an exhibition *Liquid Crystals in Art* at the Lamda Theatre Club in London for which a broadsheet and poster were produced. On 2 October 1970, for the *Metzger Retrospective* at the National Film Theatre 2 in London, the artist showed film, slides and a selection of his light projections. The seats were covered in newspapers in order to provoke a happening at the start.

The moment when Metzger's liquid crystal projections reached a wider audience came in December 1966 when Metzger was invited to demonstrate this technique for concerts given by Cream, The Who and The Move at the Roundhouse in London. The process was very labour-intensive, and twelve assistants operated twelve projectors.

For the first time, a fully mechanised, environmental version of this work will be presented at the Museum of Modern Art Oxford in autumn 1998, created with the assistance of Adrian Fogarty, an electronic engineer. The fully automated projectors will be fixed with a heating/cooling device and a rotating polarized filter,

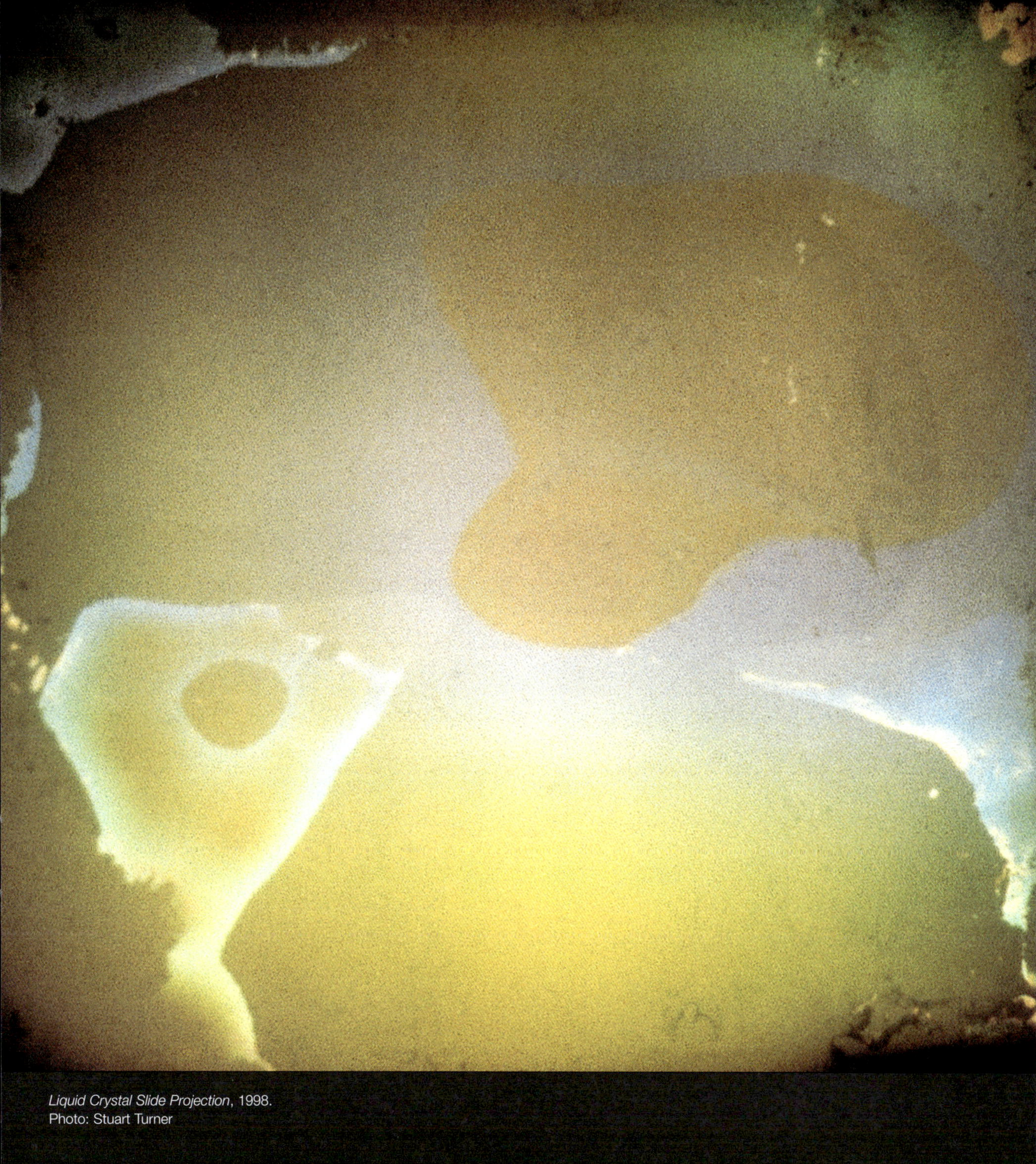

Liquid Crystal Slide Projection, 1998.
Photo: Stuart Turner

ART OF LIQUID CRYSTALS

A new art technique is on view in a window of Better Books (corner of Charing Cross Road and New Compton Street)

Two aspects of the technique are displayed:

1. as the spectator passes pieces of glass mounted in the window, a series of colour changes may be observed

2 a chemical is mounted between microscope cover slips. In the course of a one-minute cycle, the chemical is melted and then cooled. As the chemical cools, colour changes are observed which vary according to the position of the spectator and the light source. This work is called EARTH FROM SPACE

The technique is based on the use of liquid crystals. It can be used on a large scale, inside buildings or out. The exhibit is the work of Gustav Metzger. He is the author of AUTO-DESTRUCTIVE ART - the first illustrated monograph on the subject, published in October 1965

An evening on auto-destructive and auto-creative art will be held at Better Books on 8th January, Saturday at 9 p m. Speakers include Frank Popper of Paris, a leading authority on kinetic art.

The PRESS is invited to view the exhibit in the window of Better Books on Thursday 6th January between 11 and 12 or between 2 and 3, when Mr Metzger will be present

For further information please phone TEM 6944

Press release for
Art of Liquid Crystals,
January, 1966

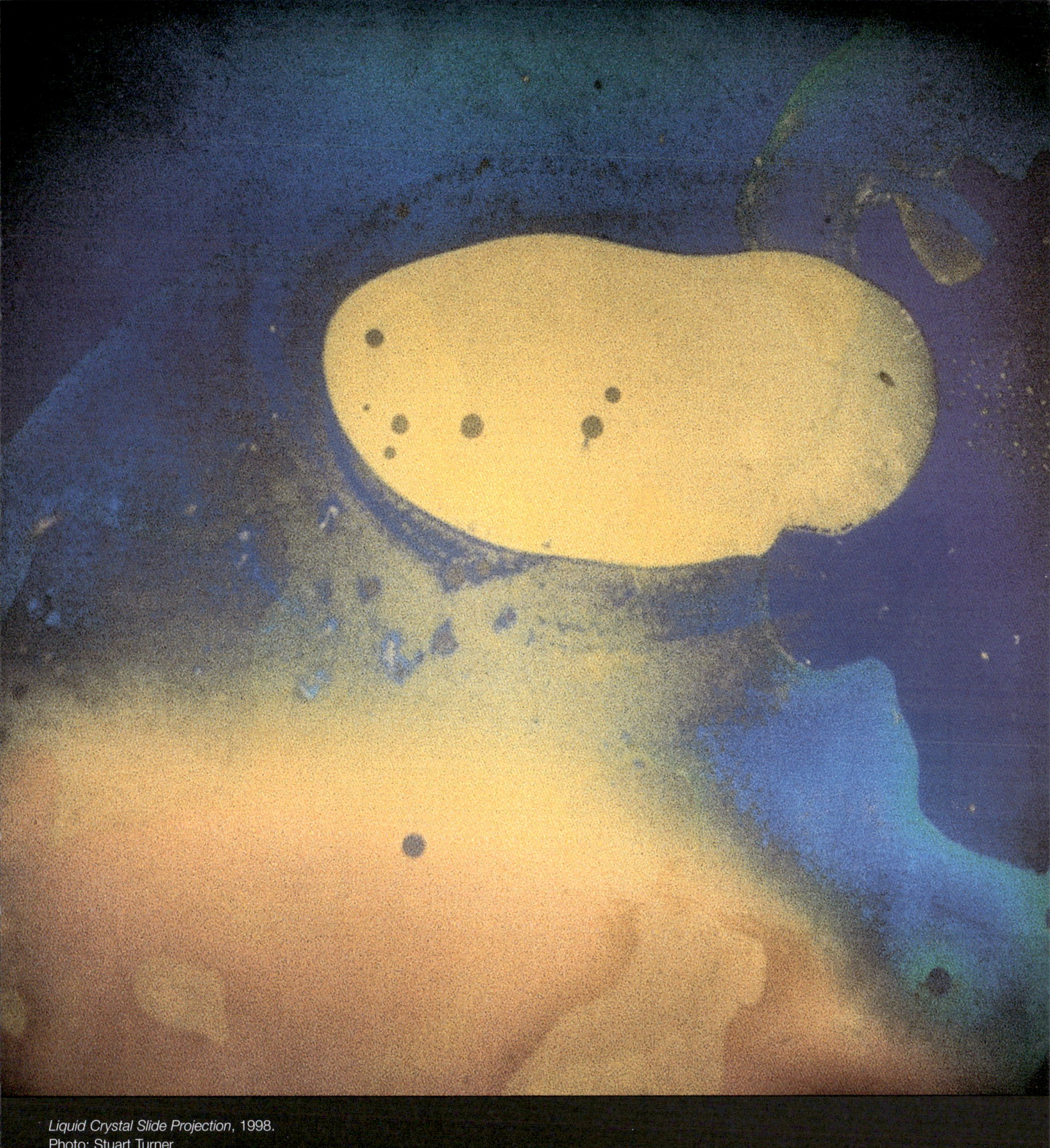

Liquid Crystal Slide Projection, 1998.
Photo: Stuart Turner

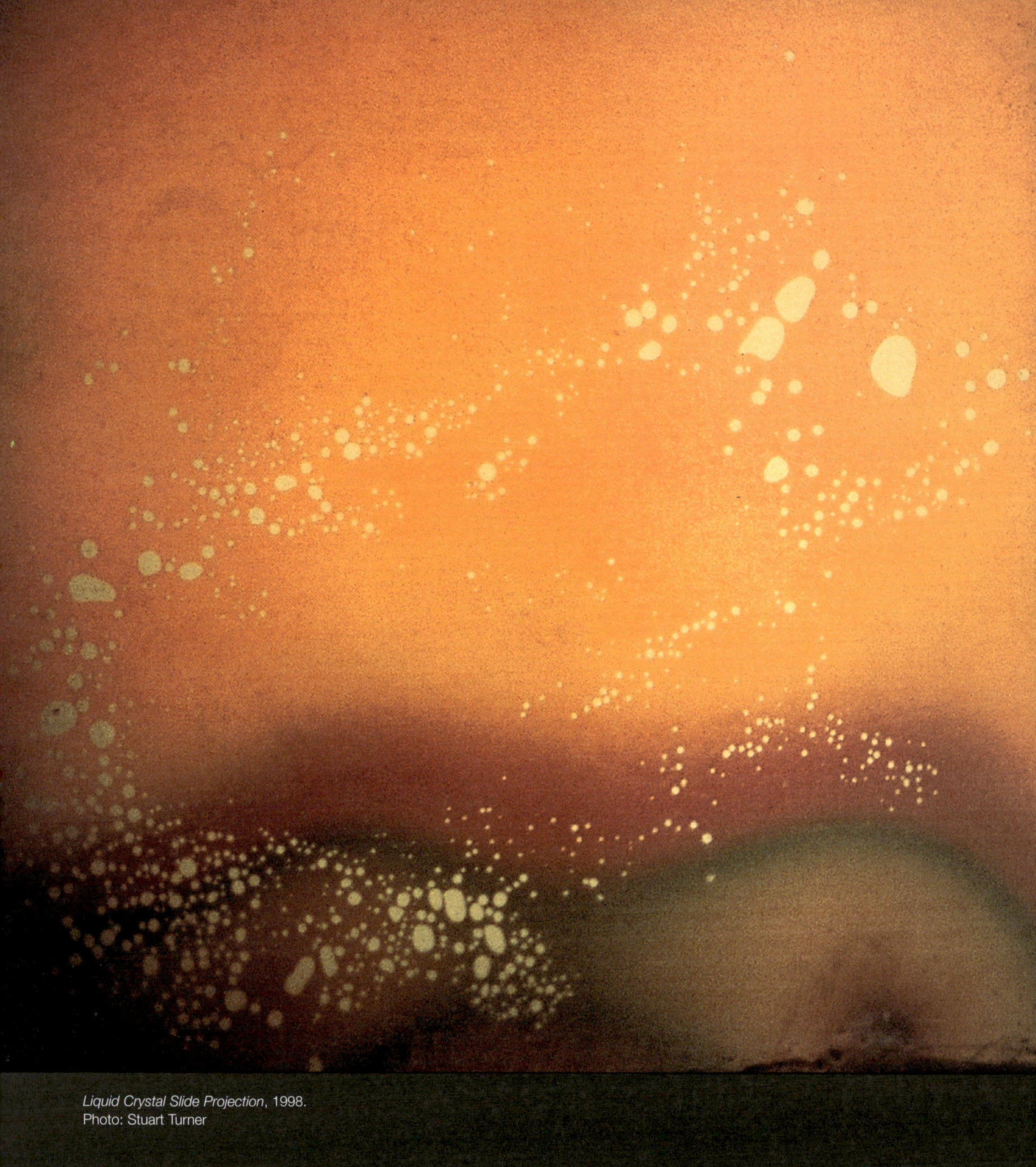

Liquid Crystal Slide Projection, 1998.
Photo: Stuart Turner

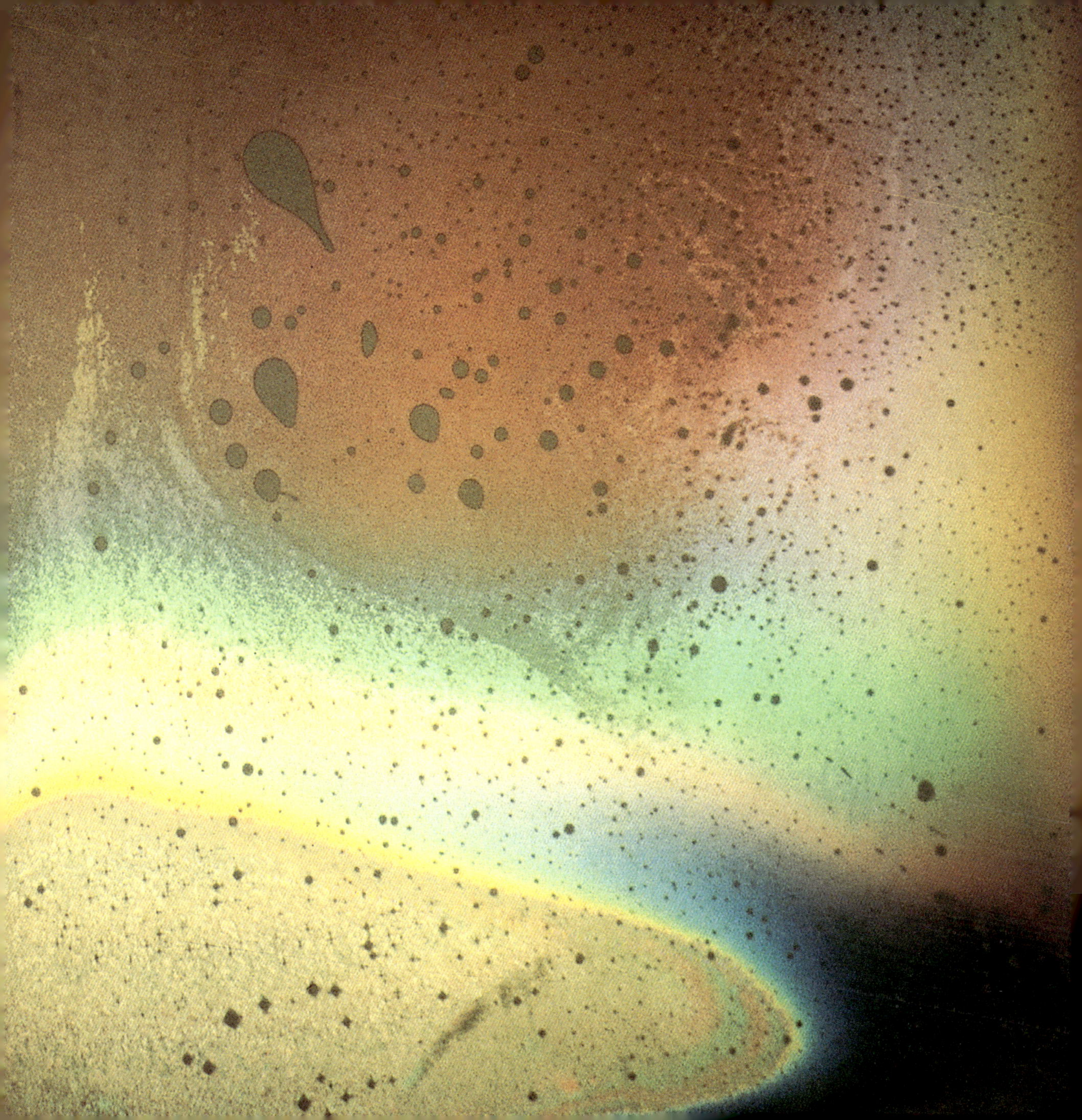

programmed by computer to start at different times. This will result in six different projectors all displaying the liquid crystal effect simultaneously. Metzger has likened the resulting sweeps of colour to those of a Turner landscape or paintings by Mark Rothko.

With this *Liquid Crystal Environment* in Oxford, it would seem that finally the ideals set out in the words of the 1961 manifesto had been achieved: 'Auto-destructive art and auto creative art aim at the integration of art with the advances of science and technology. The immediate objective is the creation, with the aid of computers,of works of art whose movements are programmed and include 'self-regulation'.'

Metzger intends the environment to have a very calming effect on the viewer, an important and necessary emotional counterbalance to the other large installation of the exhibition, the *Historic Photographs.* It will be a space suitable for quiet meditation, where live music events could also be performed.

Extremes Touch: Material/Transforming Art, Swansea Arts Festival, 1968

The other manifestations of Gustav Metzger's Auto Creative Art came in an exhibition he co-ordinated at the Filtration Laboratory in the Department of Chemical Engineering at the University College of Swansea in Wales as part of the Swansea Arts Festival of 1968. Metzger showed six kinetic sculptures in this exhibition for which he also wrote an accompanying text listing the combined mechanical and natural elements employed to make the works. One consisted of a found rectangular polystyrene sheet held in constant suspension by compressed air directed at the floor underneath the corners of the sheet, and in so doing, making the polystyrene sheet float.

Another sculpture, which Metzger has since called *Mica and Air Cube*, was a perspex cube filled with flakes of mica, a naturally occurring mineral, into which a constant stream of compressed air was fed through a tube. The mica circulated continually by the compressed air. Movement and ramdomness, two key elements in Metzger's work, were at play here.

Another sculpture was also shown, *Drop on Hot Plate*, 1968 comprising a hot plate supported by a metal rod. Water descended in a plastic tube, emitting a controlled drop on to the hot plate. The drop was held in a constant state of being, a blob of water held by the interaction of evaporation and the rate the water fed through.

Projects Realised and Unrealised, 1970 and 1971

Between the years 1970 and 1971 Metzger designed a series of ambitious public art projects of auto-creative and auto-destructive art for London, only some of which were realised.

One was a large scale liquid crystal projection which would project against a side wall of the Royal Festival Hall on the South Bank. Another called for a giant stack of newspapers which would pack the entire space of one of the arches under Waterloo Bridge from the ground upwards. The final project proposed was for the River Thames in front of the National Film Theatre whereby a sheet of metal would be kept in a constantly floating state. Although the feasibility study for this project was undertaken with the sponsorship of Alistair McAlpine, and given the approval of the river authorities, all these projects except the river project were rejected by the Greater London Council.

Project for Documenta 5

Metzger was invited to participate in the 1972 *documenta* 5 in Kassel, Germany. His project, *KARBA 1970/72*, which was accepted was described as follows: 'the exhausts of four cars are to be led into a 3 × 3 metre clear plastic cube for the duration of the exhibition.' The intention was that the cube would eventually become black with the fumes from the exhaust and was a clear statement about Metzger's views about pollution and the destruction of the natural world, a subject which was to re-emerge many more times in his work.[17] The project for *documenta 5* was never realised although the proposed site, in front of the Neue Galerie, was marked on the plan of the *documenta* catalogue which illustrated the whole project. The artist made a model of this work titled *Project Stockholm June*, 1972.

In 1992 Metzger produced a variant of this work in a model for *Earth Minus Environment*, a project proposed for the United Nations Earth Summit in Rio de Janeiro. The model used 120 toy cars and was shown at Harry Ruhe's Galerie A. in Amsterdam.

Art into Society/Society into Art and the 'Years without Art', 1977–1980

In 1974 Metzger was invited by the organisers Christos Joachimides and Norman Rosenthal to paricipate in the group exhibition *Art into Society/Society into Art: Seven German Artists*, at the Institute of Contemporary Art in London from

ARTS FESTIVAL '68

UNIVERSITY COLLEGE OF SWANSEA

EXTREMES TOUCH

MATERIAL/TRANSFORMING ART

CO-ORDINATED BY GUSTAV METZGER

In Filtration Laboratory, 294. Department of Chemical Engineering.

22nd January - 4th February, 1968.

Open Sunday to Friday 12 - 2, 4 - 6, Saturday 12 - 6.

Open to the public. Approached from main entrance of Applied Science block, signs guide to exhibition on the second floor.

The exhibition is arranged by the Arts Festival '68 Committee (Chairman: John Plant), with the assistance of the departments of Metallurgy, Chemical Engineering, Physics, Chemistry, and Electrical Engineering.

It is not possible to show all techniques in one period.
Exhibits marked in red are either hot or cold. Approach with care.

NO SMOKING

Materials and techniques employed. Water - jet, fall, atomized.

Main line compressed air. Floating structures. Liquid crystal phenomena

with electronically controlled continuous melting and cooling phases, - in

reflected light, and with projected polarized light. Expanded metal. Vacuum.

Nylon, copper, rubber and plastic tubes. Mica. Hot plates. Fibre optics.

Carbon dioxide. Liquid nitrogen. Dewar. Silicones. Polyethylene oxide.

Stroboscope. Graphite. Plastics. Hot air blower. Sound.

"Driven along in an incessant but variable movement some (atoms) bounce far apart after a collision while others recoil only a short distance from the impact . . . . . those that do not recoil far being driven into a closer union and held there by the entanglement of their own interlocking shapes . . ."
Lucretius.
Quoted on page 116 - L. S. Penrose, "Automatic Mechanical Self-Reproduction".
In New Biology, No. 28 Penguin Books, London, 1959.

Exhibition statement for *Extremes Touch: Material/Transforming Art*, Swansea Arts Festival, 1968

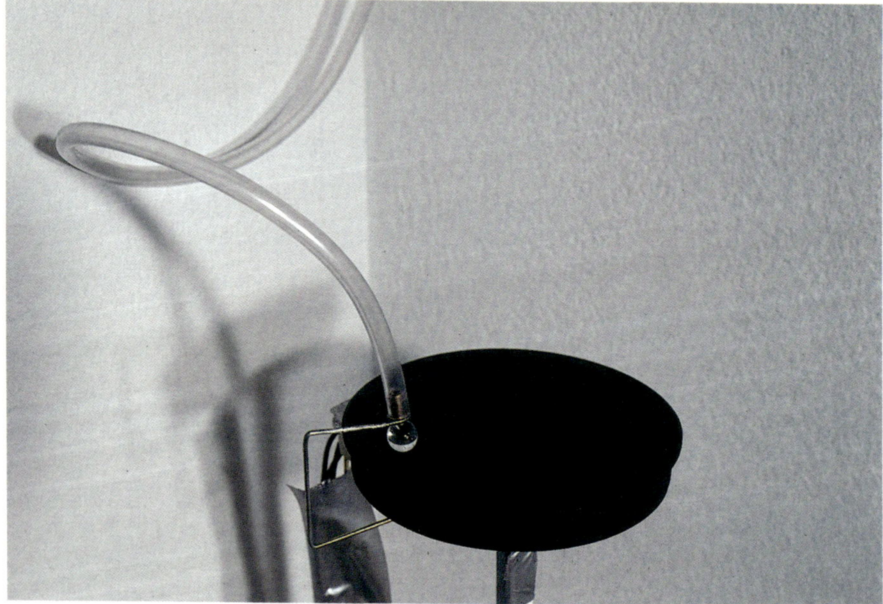

Drop on Hot Plate, 1968/98 work in progress at the exhibition *Speed* Whitechapel Gallery, London 1998. Photo: Mark Hakansson

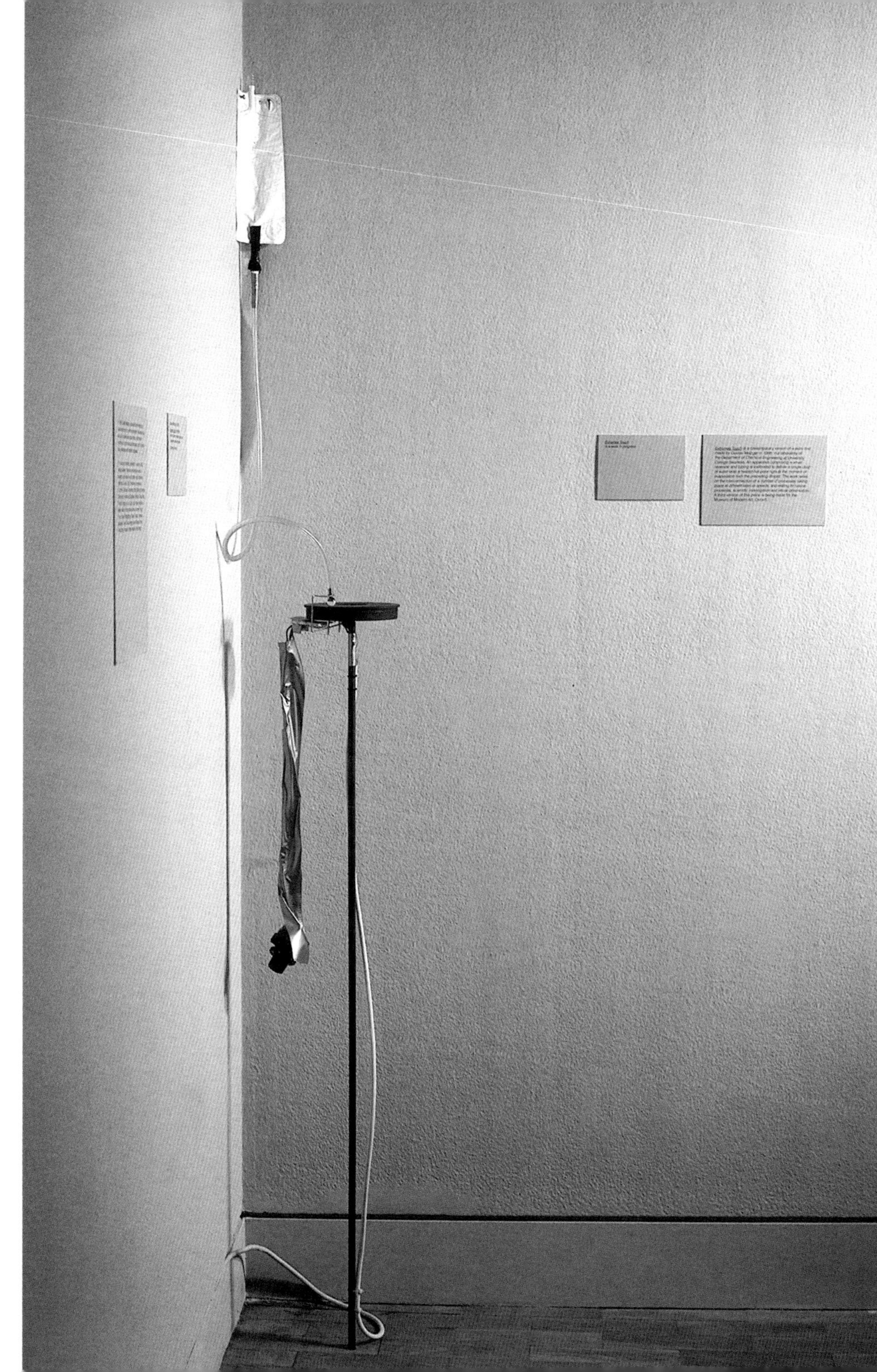

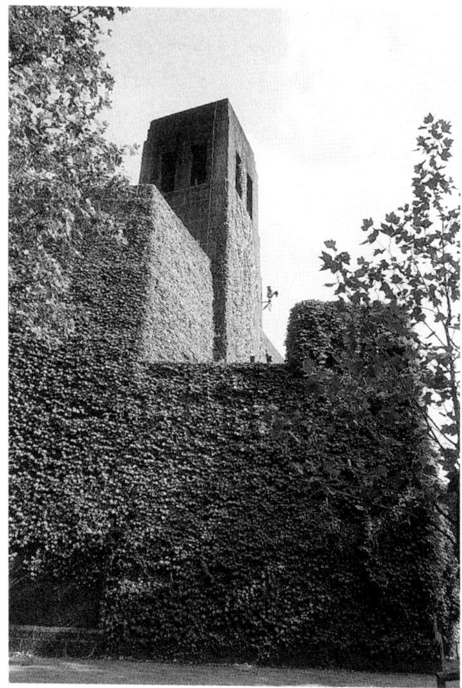

Projects Realised I
1972/98
[The Citadel, London].
Photo:
Bartholomew Dudley

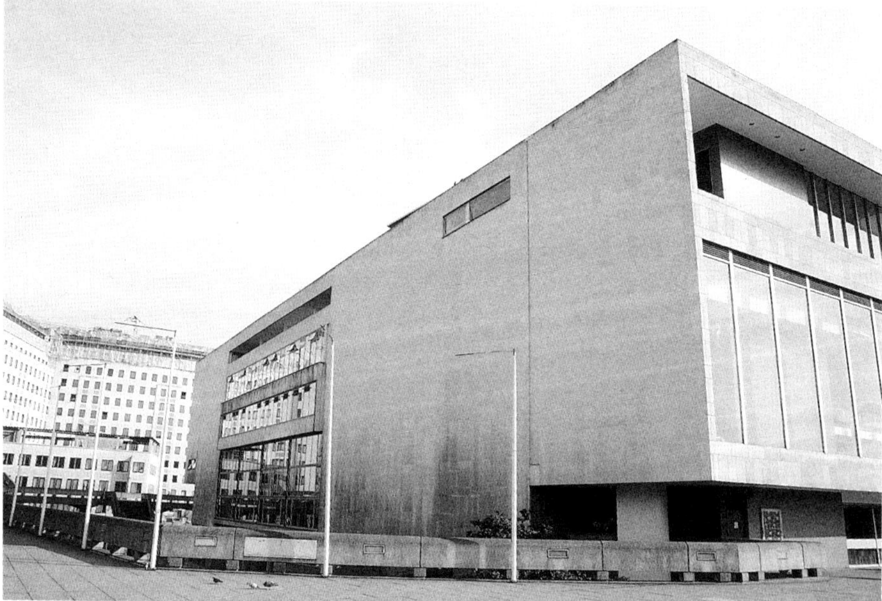

Projects Unrealised I
1972/98
[Royal Festival Hall, London].
Photo:
Bartholomew Dudley

30 October to 24 November but he decided not to exhibit. Coming after what had been for Metzger a particularly busy period, Metzger had become disillusioned with what he saw as the increasing commercialisation of art and conveyed his feelings in the catalogue by making a statement calling for 'Years Without Art, 1977–1980'. In this he urged artists to give up producing and showing work altogether for three years, not merely as a gesture of protest against the commodification of art but as an opportunity for artists to reflect and engage more in theoretical activity. Again, he was to be alone in this project, and felt that his intentions were misunderstood. A comprehensive account is given by Justin Hoffmann in his foreword to the publication *Gustav Metzger Manifeste Schriften Konzepte*.[18]

The 1990s and Historic Photographs, 1995–98

After having virtually withdrawn from the artworld in the 1980s, Metzger's activities in the latter half of the 1990s, could not have been in greater contrast, and have proven to be one of the most productive periods of his career. Since 1995, he has had two books published, one in German; he has had two small one person exhibitions; he has recorded two video interviews with influential art critics; his work has been acquired by major international collections and he has shown works in three international exhibitions.

Within this time, the most significant moment in Metzger's artistic development came with a series of work which he has called *Historic Photographs*.

For some time Metzger had been contemplating the position and role of the spectator in art, which he was eventually to expound in a lecture he gave at Hanbury Street Hall, titled *The Exclusion of the Spectator in Art* on 31 January 1996.

Metzger's three-dimensional *Historic Photographs* works have grown out of his continued fascination with the power of the press photograph and the way in which these capture pivotal and tragic moments in modern history; to be more presise, within the history defined by his own lifetime, and which exemplify man's capacity for destruction – the Holocaust, the Vietnam War, the conflict between the Israelis and Palestinians; terrorism and the destruction of nature. His source material – photographs taken originally for newspapers and magazines, seem to define these moments and come to acquire an almost iconic status, by being shown and repeated again and again, often ending up in history books, films and videos.

Such is the importance of these subjects to Metzger that he does not want to make it too easy for the viewer to see the image. Accordingly, he obscures the image with covers made of materials which in some way echo the subject of the

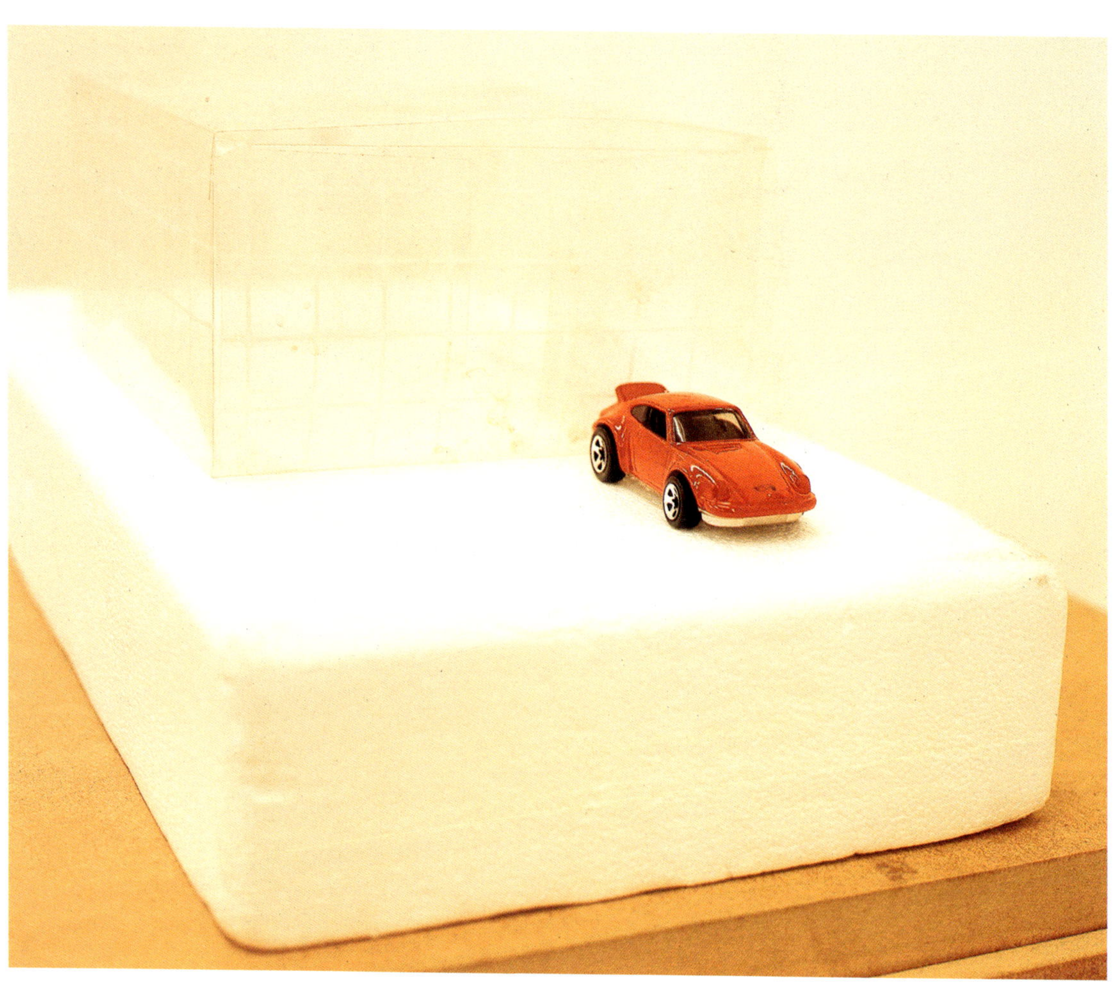

Project 'Stockholm June' 1972, detail, 1997.
Photo: Pia Lanzinger

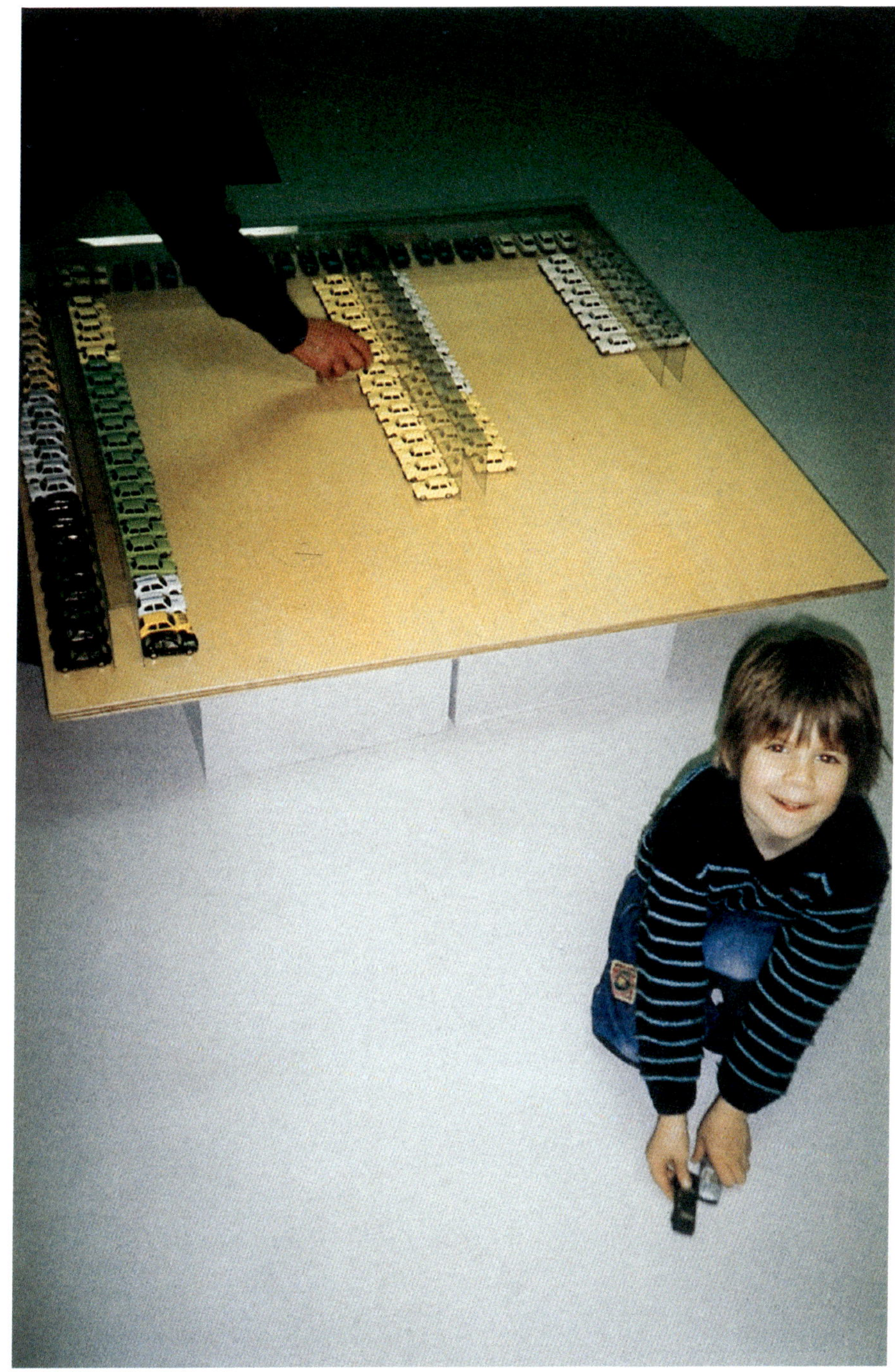

Earth Minus Environment, Amsterdam, spring 1992. Model with 120 toy cars

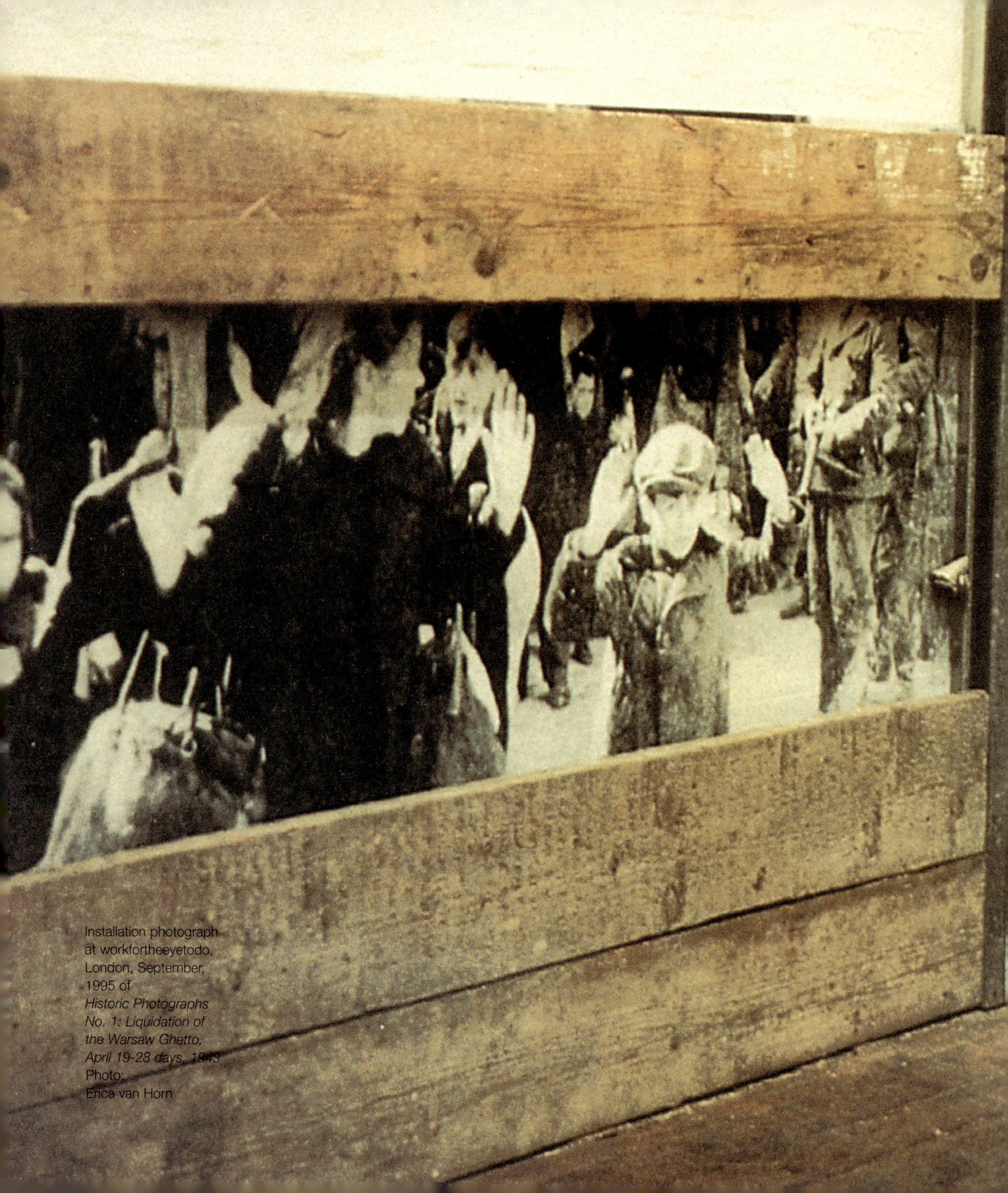

Installation photograph at workfortheeyetodo, London, September, 1995 of *Historic Photographs No. 1: Liquidation of the Warsaw Ghetto, April 19-28 days, 1943* Photo: Erica van Horn

GUSTAV METZGER

The Exclusion of the Spectator in Art

a talk on Wednesday 31st January 1996 at 7.30pm in

Hanbury Street Hall
22A Hanbury St. London E1

and afterwards at *workfortheeyetodo*
51 Hanbury St. London E1 0171 426 0579
for the publication of *Damaged Nature, Auto-destructive Art* by Gustav Metzger

Announcement card for the lecture *The Exclusion of the Spectator in Art*, London, 1996

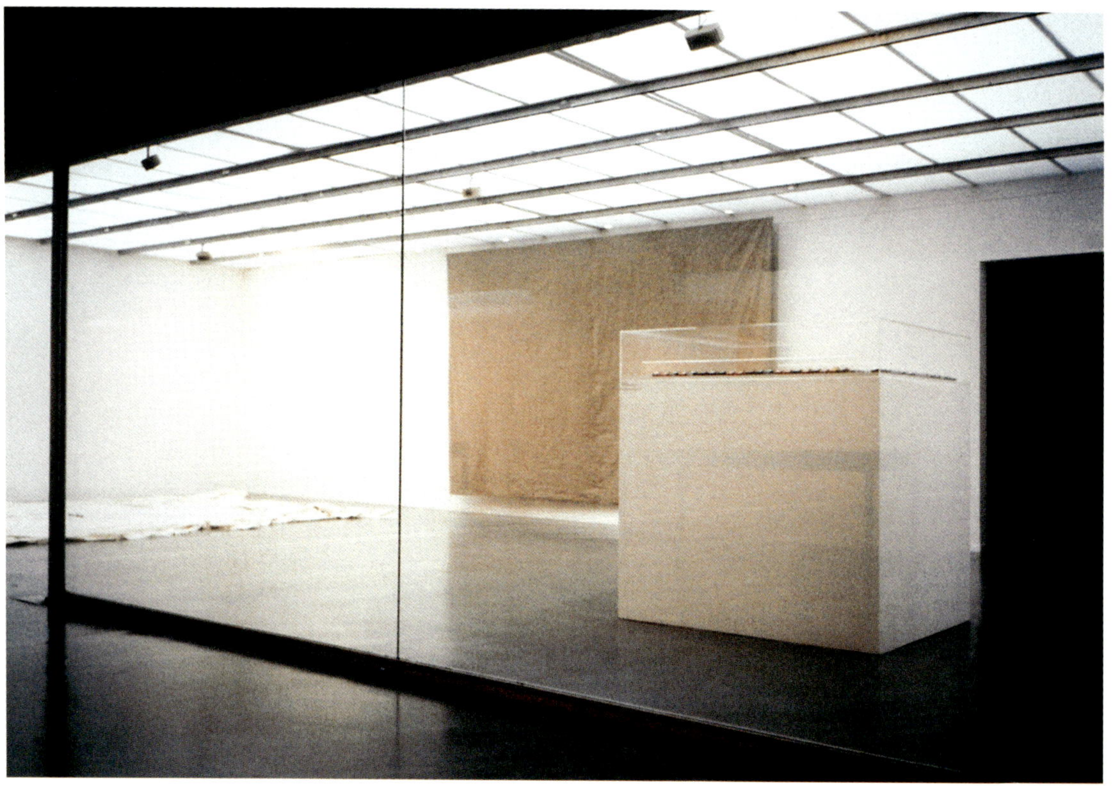

Gustav Metzger's installation at the *Life/Live* exhibition at the Musée d'Art Moderne de la Ville de Paris, 1996

photograph. For Metzger, the challenge presented to the spectator is crucial; these works demand a new interaction, both mental and physical, in order to fully experience them. Some pieces are literally 'to crawl into' or 'to walk into', the reality of the subject within the photograph becoming an all-engulfing reality to the viewer.

These are works that respond to a physically and socially changing world; the reality to which Metzger constantly returns. As Gustav Metzger and I sat together, examining and selecting the material for this book from the pile of assorted documents, letters, press clippings, faded manifestos, manuscripts, journals and just a few photographs (most of which have been collected by former collaborators and friends), he turned to me and said, 'well this is it, this is my life. If I ever write an an autobiography I will call it "A Footnote in History"', an appropriate title for a man who has spent a lifetime observing reality from the margins and whose relevance and influence within the history of British Art has only begun to be fully appreciated in his later years.

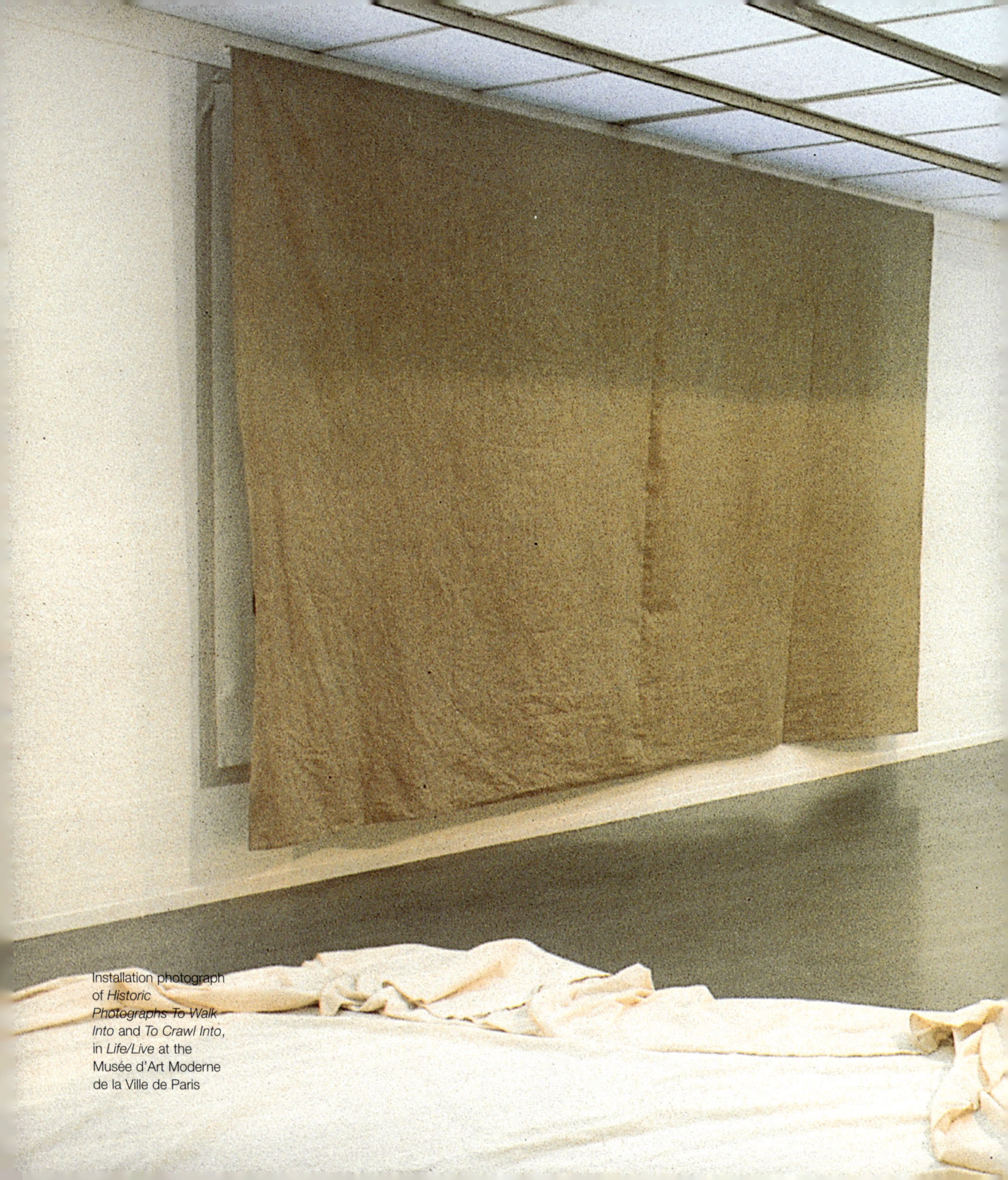

Installation photograph of *Historic Photographs To Walk Into* and *To Crawl Into*, in *Life/Live* at the Musée d'Art Moderne de la Ville de Paris

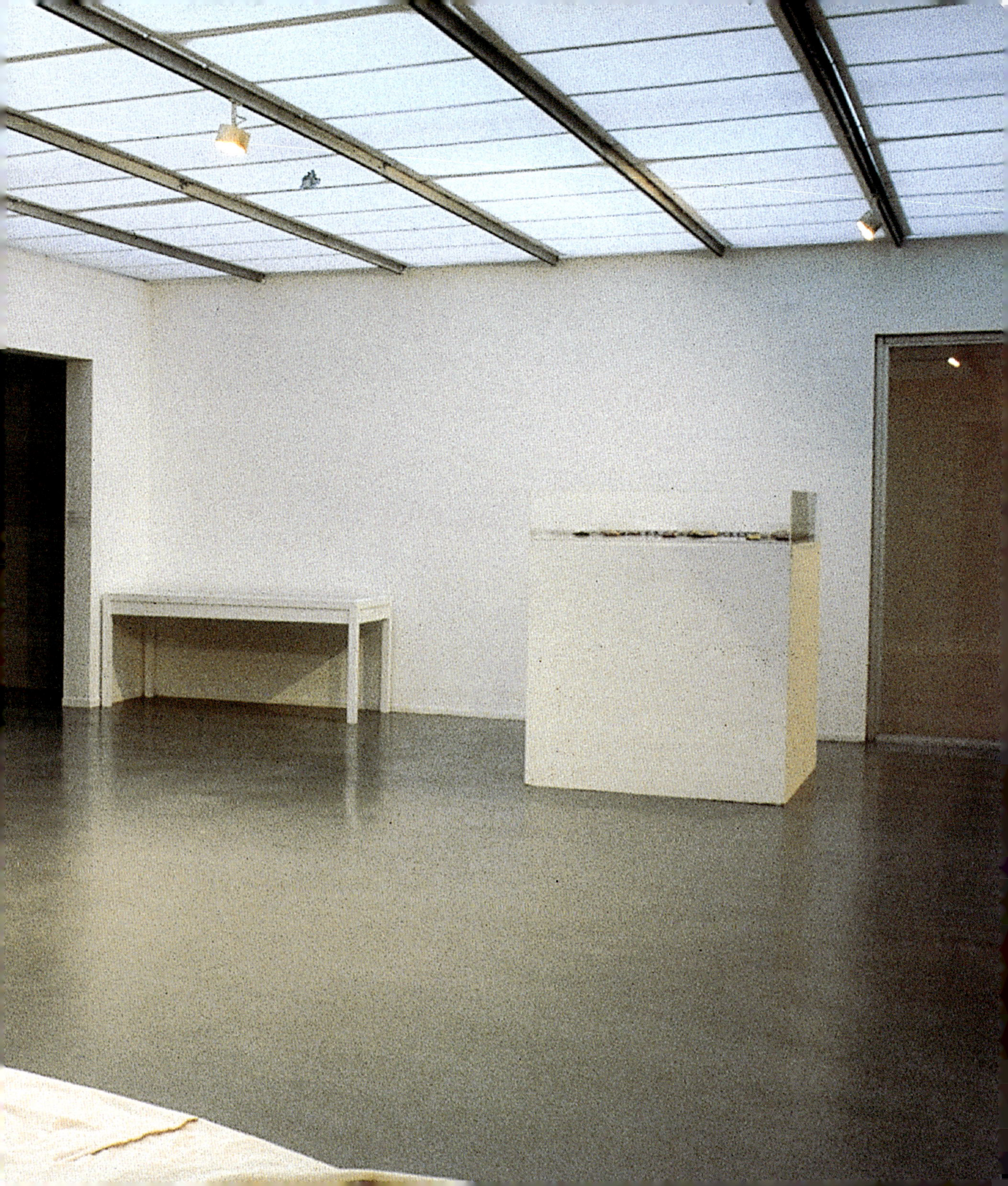

1
Clive Phillpot, for the publication *Gustav Metzger 'Damaged Nature, Auto-Destructive Art'*, Coracle @ workfortheeyetodo, London, in 1996, compiled a meticulous chronology of the artist's life and work, which has been the basis of much of the factual information in this essay.

2
Gustav Metzger in a video interview with Andrew Wilson, London, January 1998.

3
John Rydon, 'It's Pictures from Packing Cases', *Daily Express*, London, 12 November 1959.

4
Gustav Metzger's untitled 1996 statement on *Cardboards* is reprinted in *Gustav Metzger: Manifeste, Schriften, Konzepte*, Verlag Silke Schreiber, München, 1997, p. 99.

5
The new line was inserted in pencil by Metzger on an original copy of the first manifesto and is now part of the collection of the Archiv Sohm, Staatsgalerie, Stuttgart.

6
See John A. Walker, 'Message from the Margin', *Art Monthly*, London, October 1995, pp. 14–17.

7
ibid.

8
'Miles interviews Pete Townshend', *International Times*, London, 13 February 1967.

9
'Four Manifestoes by Gustav Metzger', *Signals Newsbulletin of the Centre for Advanced Creative Study London*, vol. 1, no. 2, September 1964, p. 14.

10
Auto-Destructive Art, Metzger at AA, ACC, London, June 1965.

11
Kristine Stiles, whose unpublished PhD thesis was on DIAS, has written extensively about the subject, including her essay 'Uncorrupted Joy: International Art Actions', *in Out of Actions: between performance and the object, 1949–1979*, p. 272–273.

12
Art and Artists, 'Auto Destructive' special issue, August 1966.

13
Letter to Ivor Davies, 18 August, 1966.

14
See Stiles in *Out of Actions*, p. 274.

15
Arthur Moyse, *Freedom*, September 1966.

16
Op cit.

17
See Gustav Metzger's essay 'Nature demised resurrects as environment' in Gustav Metzger, *Damaged Nature, Auto-Destructive Art*, Coracle, London, 1996.

18
Justin Hoffmann, 'Gustav Metzger – real underground', *Gustav Metzger, Manifeste Schriften Konzepte*, Verlag Silke Schreiber, München, 1997, pp. 7–12.

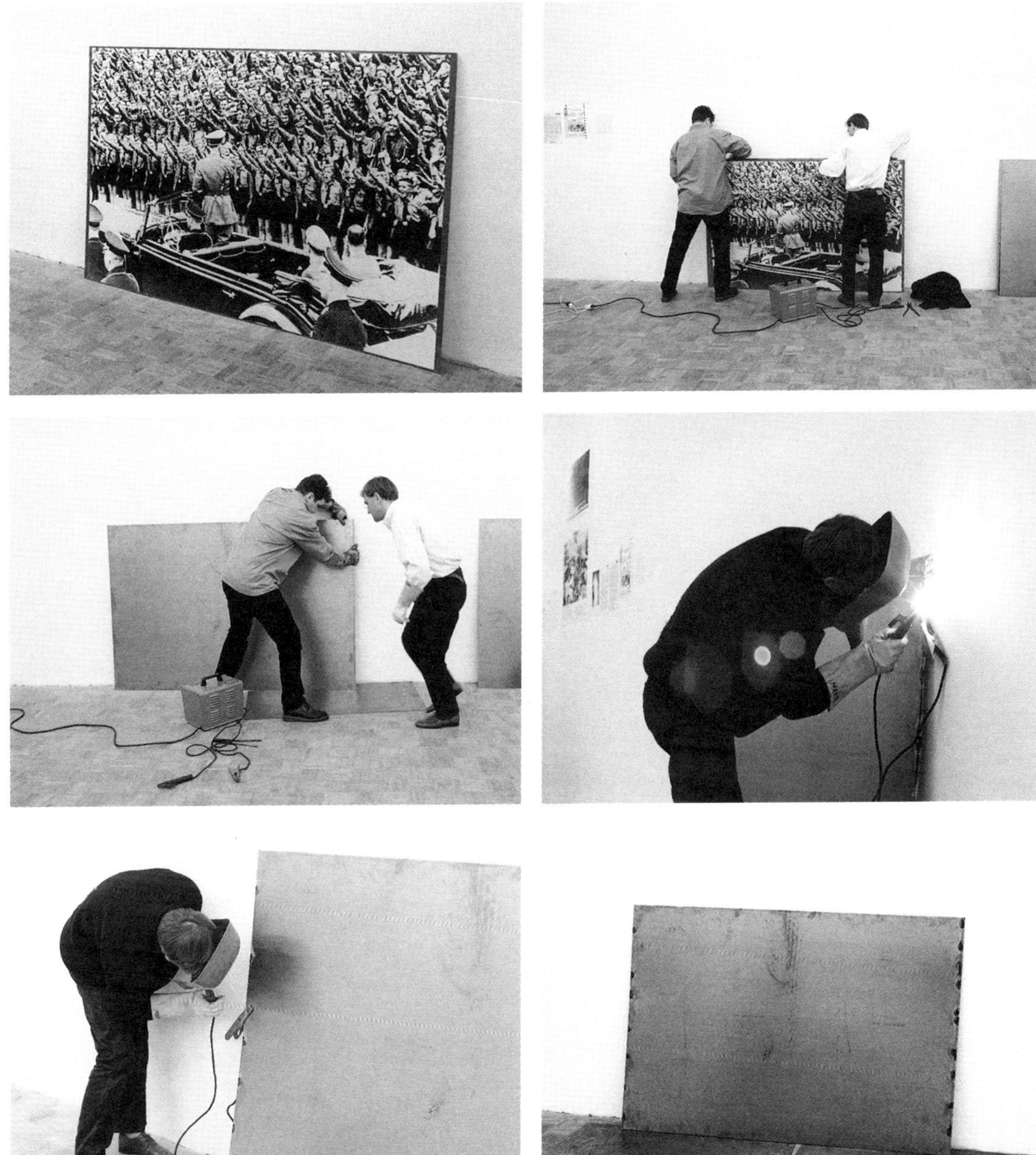

Welding of *Historic Photographs: Hitler-Youth, Eingeschweisst*, 1997 at the Kunstraum, München, 11 September 1997.
Photo: Pia Lanzinger

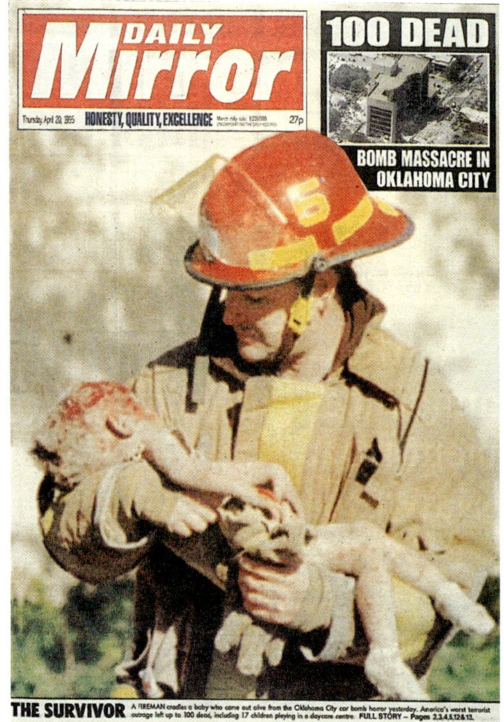

DAILY Mirror

Thursday, April 20, 1995 HONESTY, QUALITY, EXCELLENCE 27p

100 DEAD

BOMB MASSACRE IN OKLAHOMA CITY

THE SURVIVOR A FIREMAN cradles a baby who came out alive from the Oklahoma City car bomb horror yesterday. America's worst terrorist outrage left up to 100 dead, including 17 children playing in a daycare centre. FULL STORY – Pages 2,3,4,5,12&13.

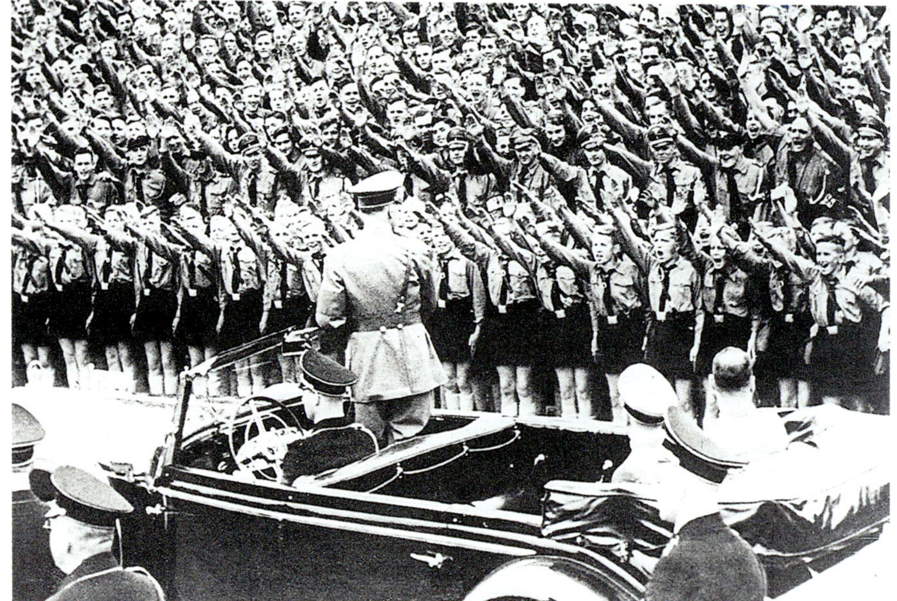

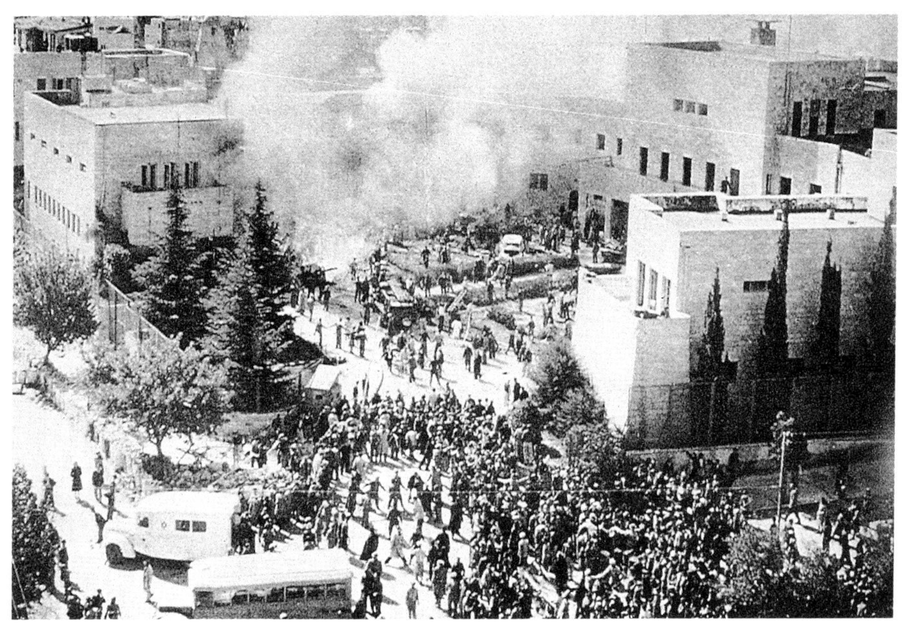

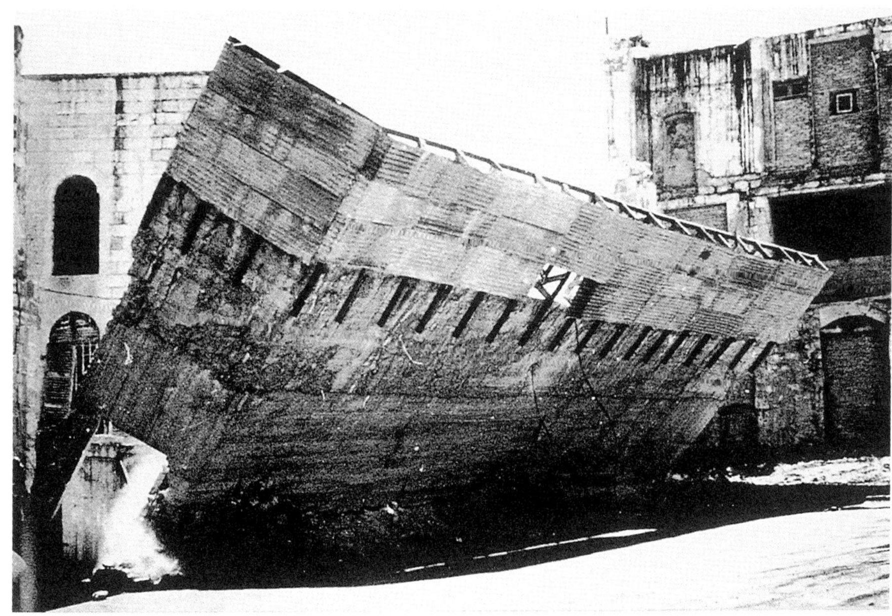

Source material for
Historic Photographs

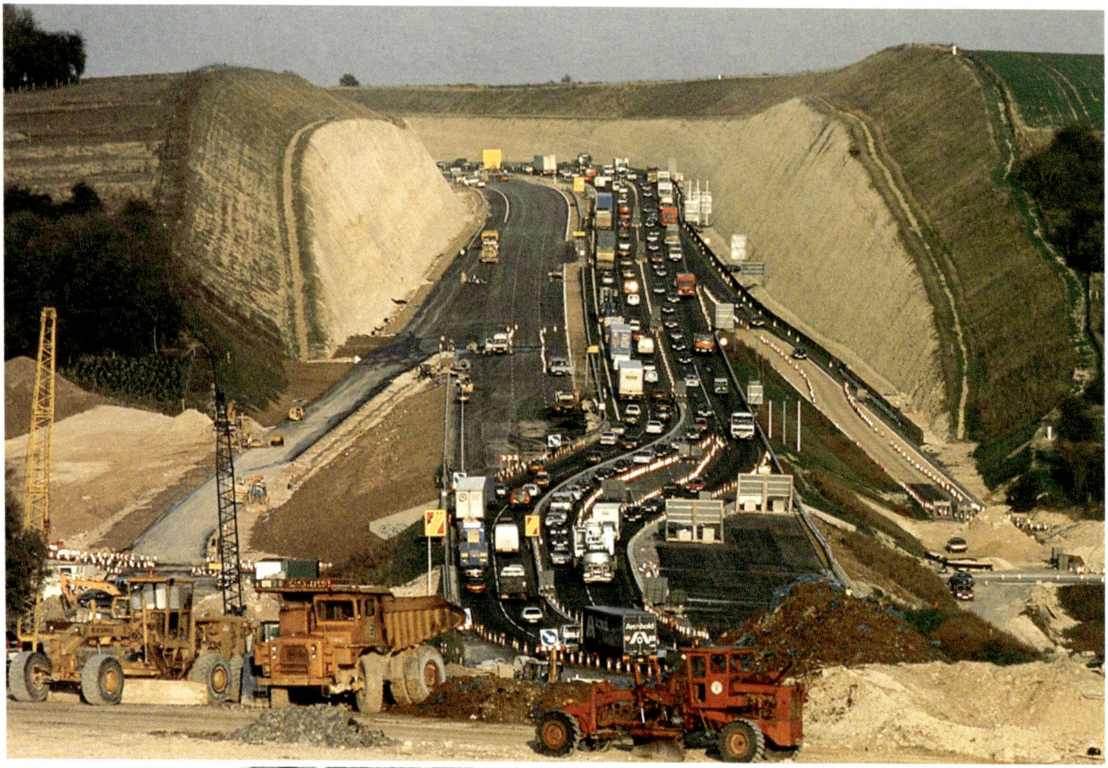

Photo: Steve Morgan

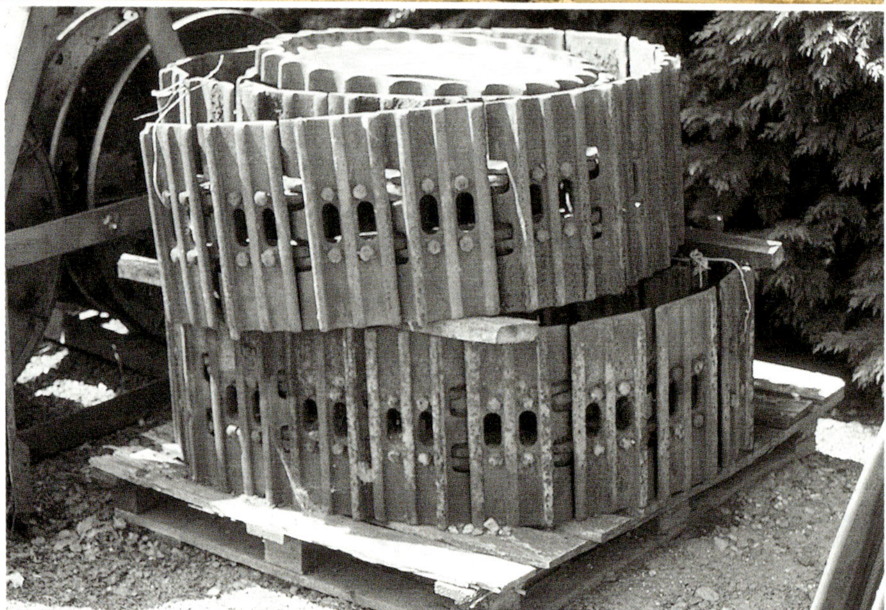

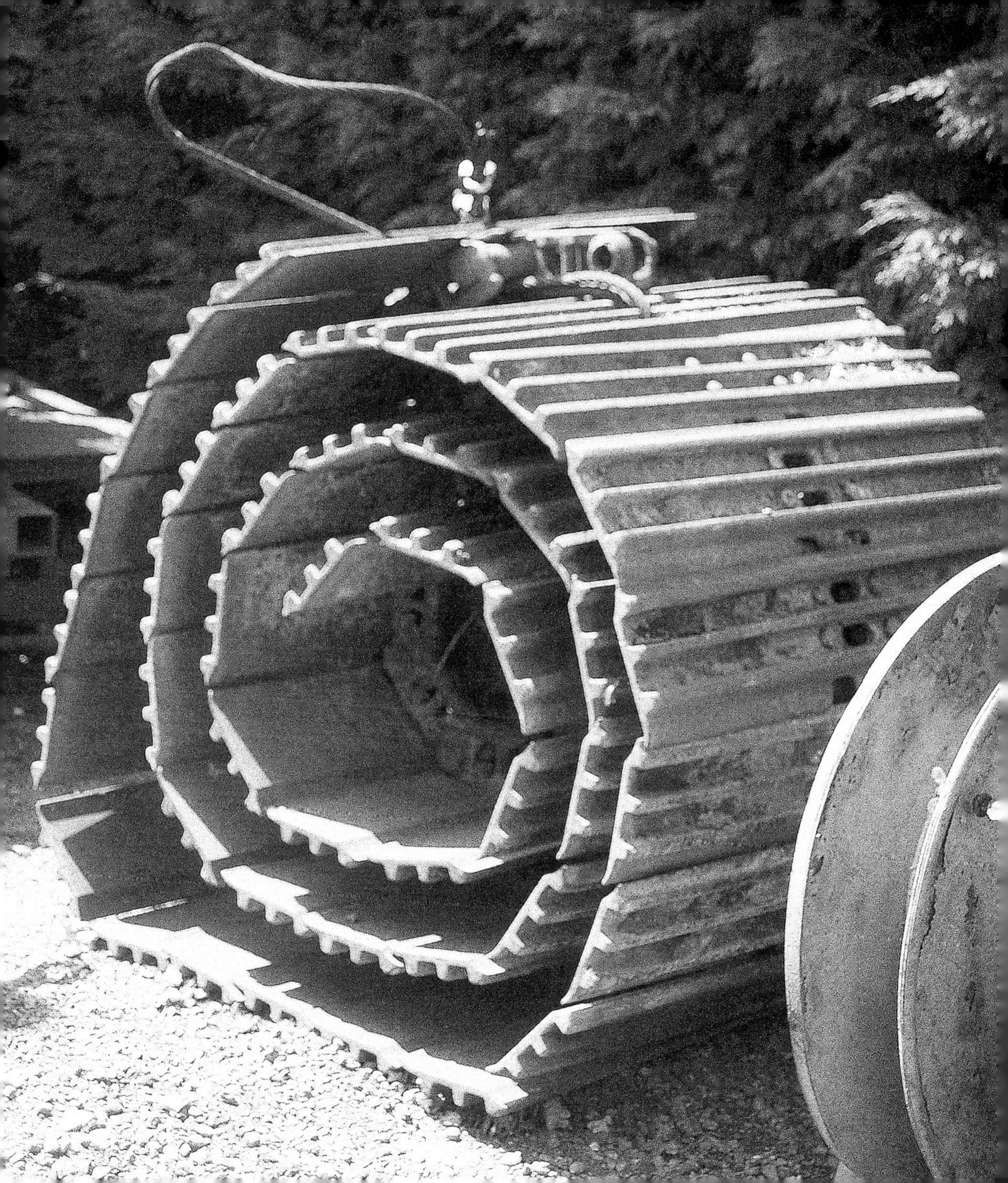

Gustav Metzger – The Artist as a Wanderer

Norman Rosenthal

The evolution of Gustav Metzger's persona and art represents, in a British context especially, a continually developing rhetorical question as to where lies the most central concern of art and its relationship to society at large. Is it in the production of the consumable art object, which gives value above all to the individual artist's technique applied to a given subject matter whether in drawing or painting? Is it one of the myriad methods by which a three-dimensional art object is made and possibly reproduced? Or is it in the dissemination of ideas given some kind of imaginative visual form, however elusive, by means only of the spoken or written word? Does the artist exist merely like a hermit monk unconnected, on the surface at least, to the outside world? Is his role that of a prophet imaginatively warning of the fragility of experience and of phenomena both natural and above all man-made? 'Art for art's sake', wrote P.J. Proud'hon, the great French anarchist, writer and philosopher friend of Courbet, in 1865,' is a debauch of the heart and dissolution of the spirit' and although many, though not all, artists might agree with him, few have not compromised themselves in the face of such simple ideas, usually in the interests of production and the market. Metzger, however, has squarely faced this fundamental existential question, the paradoxes that lie within it, and over a career spanning more than fifty years has made it his business continually to renew his answers in the face of developments in Art, Science and the body politic at large. Above all, he has accepted the consequences of these answers to his questions.

His aspect, certainly since he abandoned painting in the Fifties, having been a favoured student of David Bomberg, has been that of a prophet, often one of impending doom. His very appearance is that of a latter day Old Testament Sage. His eyes shine with a piercing intensity as he addresses those he meets, a wanderer who roams the world, or rather the streets, carrying his whole life in bags almost as large as himself, full of books and papers. He appears to have no permanent home, although now he is based mainly in London. In recent years he has been on the move, around Europe, largely in Germany, Switzerland and Holland – almost completely removed from the community of the world of art. Most had forgotten him, but to an increasing circle he is acquiring the status of a living legend, an innovator, whose gentle but decisive actions have born much fruit in the minds and production of generations of British Artists, whether they were directly aware of him or not. Now that he has reached past the biblical age of three score years and ten, he has been increasingly thinking that it might be worth making art again, as well as just reflecting on it.

History and the stresses inherent in contemporary society bear down on all of us, but Metzger has been highly sensitive to those stresses, perhaps for reasons explicable by his own early history. Born in Nürnberg, of Orthodox Polish-Jewish parentage, he grew up in the midst of the unspeakable dangers and terrors of National Socialism. It was that terror that unwillingly propelled him and his brother, as it did a number of others, including for example Frank Auerbach, to England as part of a child rescue operation. They were then separated from the rest of his family, his mother and father, who met their deaths in concentration camps in Poland, which he escaped by a hair's breadth's accident of history. Now, half a century later, Metzger can look back, carrying with him that agonised sense of guilt that is the lot of all survivors, on a lifetime largely spent drawing precise attention to the endless potential of mass destruction, military and environmental, and as an artist constantly inventing strategies to look directly at horrors both potential and real that have come to haunt our century and which seem certain to spill over into the next with increasing ferocity.

Art comes from art, and yet the power of an individual artist, like the scientist, lies permanently in his or her ability to innovate and to pass on new ideas and forms that can be transformed and be given further life in the work of other artists. Taking much from Bomberg, who in his own youth had stylistically given crucial inspiration to the radical if short-lived Vorticist Group; from Kurt Schwitters, whose late collages contained within them a sense of autodestruction; and from the early inventions of Paolozzi, Hamilton and others who came together for the *This is Tomorrow* exhibition in 1956, Metzger went on to become an artist who in an English context has played a discrete but nonetheless immensely powerful role. In its own way, it has been as significant and far-sighted as that of Joseph Beuys in Germany, of Tinguely in France and Switzerland or of Rauschenberg in the United States. If he has not achieved anything remotely like the fame of his foreign contemporaries, it is partly because of the suspicion that even now accompanies all notions of 'Expanded Art' in Britain, even in generally educated circles, to an extent that is beyond understanding in Europe and North America. But it is even more due to Metzger's own conscious decision, over the last two decades especially, to distance himself not only from the art market, but also from the art world itself as regards production and exhibitions.

It was as long ago as 1974, in an exhibition I co-organised with Christos M. Joachimides at the ICA *Art into Society – Society into Art – Seven German Artists* (the irony and ambiguity of Metzger participating, albeit reluctantly, in a German exhibition was not lost on all of us!), that Metzger signalled 'A period of three years – 1977 to 1980 – when artists will not produce work, sell work, permit work to go on exhibition and refuse collaboration with any part of the publicity machinery of the art world'. It was a culminating moment of Metzger's own carefully evolved aesthetic of revolution – a response and a sense of responsibility towards the world at large, which finally caught up with himself and with the art world – that his own development had propelled him to inhabit. Of course his call, to no-one's surprise, not least his own, was not taken up. Indeed it coincided with an ever more entwined involvement of art and artists in the newly respectable capitalist culture that surfaced around 1980 and the quantum leap in the significance of the contemporary art market that took place around that time. It was becoming, quite suddenly, increasingly common for large multinational firms to sponsor art events, including it should be added *Art into Society* itself which was part of a manifestation connected to Britain's entry into the EEC and which received partial support from the then prominent Bowater Corporation.

Was this then a case of the artist biting the hand that feeds him? Of course Metzger was as aware as anyone of the dilemma and irony facing this art exhibition, or any other, as a platform for ideas. Indeed there is a sense of deep irony and tragi-comedy in many of Metzger's interventions in the world of art. At the same time he remains desperately serious about the inherent instability and impermanence that is characteristic of the individual and the world at large. Metzger's sense of guilt as an artist stems precisely from the fact that whilst the market systems of value ceaselessly propel art towards a sense of permanence and immortality the real world and the reality of art is about inevitable decay and destruction. This is as true of the Mona Lisa as it was of the Auto-Destructive Art Demonstration on the South Bank in July 1961.

Metzger's own production – art works, publications, moments of intensive discussion – has been well documented in two recent publications, one in English, one in German, as well as this publication. At one level that production can be viewed as very limited. Apart from his as yet unseen early painting, it is only in the last two or three years that there have been works, in the ordinary sense – above all the covered photographs and the model for *Earth Minus Environment*. Even now the greater part of Metzger's work consists of proposals, manifestos, photographs and videos of actions, other archival material and above all bibliographies that act as mnemonics and guides for further study and thought. For the exhibition *Art into Society* Metzger spent weeks compiling for its catalogue a bibliography about the art market consisting of 178 separate items that included books, catalogues and learned essays as well as newspaper articles that he himself had collected. It was the bibliography that permitted him to reflect accurately on the phenomenon of the art dealer and that acted as a liberating guide for others who might be interested. Metzger had indeed appeared to survive largely as a second hand book dealer and collector, to be found haunting dusty bookshops that for him served as chaotic repositories of memories and as sources of endless information that he was for ever threatening to put in order. But a glance at his biography, so lovingly compiled by Clive Phillpot, serves to document a life that has not littered the world with an excess of production, but that has been prophetic and effective in planting ideas, like pebbles, gently cast into water.

These ripples have spread very far, provoked above all by the disturbing horror of the nuclear threat, which to Metzger clearly poses a greater threat to mankind as a whole than the worst and most barbaric excesses of Fascism. He, as is well known, found himself closely involved in the founding of the now legendary Committee of One Hundred, that was demonstrably the seed that after decades forced even Governments to act to somehow reduce the grotesque size of the nuclear stockpile, which, at its height, was sufficient to destroy life on earth many thousands of times over.

Metzger too has always been in the forefront of 'Green' ideas, ever fearful of the abuse of the earth and its natural resources by unholy alliances between scientific, economic and political interests. His own recent concept of *Damaged Nature* is a significant contribution in that it holds on to a memory of real nature that threatens to be obliterated in a mass of talk about 'Environment'.

In 1976 Metzger, with Cordula Frowein, initiated a conference on the theme of National Socialist art policies, which are only now becoming a subject of universal debate and controversy, where hitherto there had been silence. But in contemporary art too, Metzger has been far ahead of the game in a general and a specific sense. His *Cardboards* of 1959 for example anticipate Rauschenberg's explorations in the field by a decade or more. Rauschenberg's constructs of ephemera have all ultimately entered the highly controlled environment of the Market or Museum Place, with its sophisticated infrastructure of conservation that ensure the illusion of their immutability for all time. Metzger's *Cardboards* did not survive, nor were they ever meant to, although a strong memory of them survived in a *Cardboard* installation made for an exhibition at the City Racing Gallery in London in 1996. Metzger knows that, in the words of the Old Testament Prophet. 'All is vanity except the pure soul' and that all objects made by man must ultimately decay and vanish.

There is an inexorable logic in his profound sense that 'the entire span of human existence is limited, in the sense that the individual life is'. And the fact that most of us put such thoughts for the most part out of our minds in order to go on living, has enormous and unrealised consequences for the production of art, if the latter is not merely to function as an escape, a therapy or diversion from reality. That at any rate is Metzger's position and it is a valuable one in our society.

So what therefore is Metzger's position as an artist within the history of British Art? For the few that knew him well he is one of its most powerful figures of conscience. He is the gentle prophet, capable of anger in the face of what he sees as injustice, ignorance or thoughtlessness. His own mode of life in art has an exemplary quality. He is like the American composer and artist, John Cage, whose random theories profoundly influenced generations of American artists from Jasper Johns and Rauschenberg to Nauman and beyond to those who are barely aware of his existence. Metzger if anything has kept his distance from the system even more radically than Cage.

Amongst his contemporaries and those only ten or twenty years younger than himself he has through his works and interventions interacted with and profoundly influenced artists involved with kinetics and with political and conceptual art. Such figures include for instance Mark Boyle, John Latham, Peter Sedgley, David Medalla and Stuart Brisley. Equally his work has demonstrably fed into the production of artists like Victor Burgin, Richard Long, Bill Woodrow, Barry Flanagan or Bruce McLean. All these artists who have achieved prominence would probably acknowledge and be aware of Metzger as an influential figure.

But the newer generation of British Artists who have achieved such prominence in recent years know little if anything of Metzger, for in the years that they emerged Metzger had so disappeared from view as to be almost completely absent from the art world, keeping in touch spasmodically with just a few friends. But those *Sensation* artists and their contemporaries who for the most pride themselves on their apparently short cultural memories, characteristic of this generation at large, if they but knew, would quickly acknowledge Metzger as seminal a figure as any that has emerged in Britain in the last fifty years. It is the 'Sensation' generation (if such an appellation is permissible) that has most completely absorbed the ideas of destruction and damaged nature as being the essence of art. Works such as Rachel Whiteread's *House* or Damien Hirst's *Shark*, after all ironically entitled *The Physical Impossibility of Death in the Mind of Someone Living*, are spectacular physical expressions of ideas first propagated by Metzger three decades or more ago. Such affinities can also be detected in the work of artists as varied as Marc Quinn – think of his *Blood Head*; Sarah Lucas – think of her Newspaper 'Paintings'; Marcus Harvey – think of *Myra*.

Artists almost without exception 'capitalise' on their ideas and of course all steal from others. Metzger makes as small amount of capital out of his own fertile imagination as any artist of substance. His position as a non-producer would, if emulated by artists generally, to say the least be problematic. But then the question really doesn't arise. Metzger does it for all of us – he is the veritable conscience of the world of art reaching out to the rest of the world where most would fear to tread. He is the wanderer and his existence has been both necessary and valuable to all of us.

Exhibition Checklist

The following checklist is of the exhibition as presented at the Museum of Modern Art Oxford.

Cardboards
1959
photograph by John Cox (Ida Kar Studio)
26 × 24 cm
private collection, London

Auto-Destructive Art
1959
document (first manifesto)
33 × 20.5 cm
collection of the Archiv Sohm, Staatsgalerie, Stuttgart

Manifesto Auto-Destructive Art
1960
document
33 × 20.3 cm
collection of the Archiv Sohm, Staatsgalerie, Stuttgart

Auto-Destructive Art, Machine Art, Auto Creative Art
1961
document
collection of the Archiv Sohm, Staatsgalerie, Stuttgart

Model for Auto-Destructive Monument
1960/1997
staples, steel
dimensions variable
private collection, München

Daily Express
1962/98
2 newspapers
(dated 24 October 1962)
courtesy of the artist

Letters to Ivor Davies
1966
courtesy of Ivor Davies

Liquid Crystal Environment
1965/98
6 modified projectors, liquid crystal, glass slides and tubes, polaroid, computer control
dimensions variable
courtesy of the artist

Drop on Hot Plate
1968/98
hot plate, steel rod, water container, plastic tubes, water, metal tube
dimensions variable
courtesy of the artist

Mica and Air Cube
1968/98
perspex cube, mica flakes, compressed air
42 × 42 cm
courtesy of the artist

Project 'Stockholm June' 1972. Detail
1997
toy car, plastic, polystyrene
courtesy of the artist

Aprés Paolozzi PN 004886402
1997
found polystyrene object
courtesy of the artist

Projects Unrealised I
1972/98
photograph
courtesy of the artist

Projects Realised II
1972/98
photograph
courtesy of the artist

Historic Photographs No 1: Hitler addressing the Reichstag after the fall of France, July 1940
1995
photograph, MDF cover, neon lights, galvanized zinc
courtesy of the artist

Historic Photographs No. 1: Liquidation of the Warsaw Ghetto, April 19-28 days, 1943
1995
photograph, wooden shuttering, galvanized zinc
courtesy of the artist

Historic Photographs: To Walk Into, Massacre on the Mount, Jerusalem, 8 November, 1990
1996
photograph on vinyl, cloth cover
courtesy of the artist

Historic Photographs: To Crawl Into –
Anschluss, Vienna, March 1938
1996/98
photograph on foamex, cloth cover
Arts Council Collection, London

Historic Photographs: Hitler-Youth, Eingeschweisst
1997/98
photograph, 2 welded cold rolled steel sheets
courtesy of the artist

Historic Photographs: The Ramp at Auschwitz,
Summer 1944
1998
photocopy collage
courtesy of the artist

Historic Photographs: Jerusalem, Jerusalem
1998
2 photographs on 2 pvc sheets, wooden framework,
MDF boards
courtesy of the artist

Historic Photographs:
Till we have built Jerusalem
in England's green and pleasant land
1998
colour photograph on aluminium, steel caterpillar treads,
concrete slab
courtesy of the artist

Historic Photographs: Trang Bang, Children fleeing
South Vietnam, April 1972
1998
photograph on aluminium, bamboo screen, lights
courtesy of the artist

Historic Photographs: Fireman With Child,
Oklahoma, 1995
1998
photograph, breeze blocks, neon lights
courtesy of the artist

Artist's Selected Writings

The following bibliography was originally compiled by Clive Phillpot for *Gustav Metzger Damaged Nature, Auto-destructive Art*, Coracle, London, 1996 and was updated by Luise Metzel for the publication *Gustav Metzger Manifeste Schriften Konzepte*, Verlag Silke Schreiber, München,1998.

1953

Letter to *Jewish Quarterly*. Draft in David Bomberg archive, Tate Gallery Archive, London.

1957

'These artists are possessed. They gamble with life.' (Article on the Hatwell/Paolozzi/Turnbull exhibition), *King's Lynn News and Advertiser*, King's Lynn, 27 July 1956.

Old Church Art, King's Lynn Festival, 1957 (catalogue). Broadsheets on the North End Protest, King's Lynn, 1957.

1959

1st Manifesto: *Auto-Destructive Art*, 4 November 1959. Published as *Cardboards selected and arranged by G. Metzger… Auto-Destructive Art*, London, 1960. Single printed sheet with Cardboard exhibition statement preceding the manifesto.

1960

2nd Manifesto: *Manifesto Auto-Destructive Art*, 10 March 1960. Published as *Auto Destructive Art… Manifesto Auto-Destructive Art*, London, 1960. Single sheet also reprint of the 1st manifesto.

The Temple Gallery… June 1960… A New Movement in Art… London, 1960. Invitation to the first lecture-demonstration, 22 June 1960, signed by G.M. and R.C.C. Temple. (The 2nd manifesto was attached.)

1961

Bewogen Beweging, Stedelijk Museum, Amsterdam,1961. Catalogue edited by K.G. Pontus Hulten. Includes a Dutch translation of the 1st manifesto, and an illustration of the first model for auto-destructive art. The translations of the manifesto in the Danish and Swedish editions follow the Dutch edition.

3rd Manifesto: *Auto-Destructive Art, Machine Art, Auto Creative Art, 23 June 1961. Published as Auto-Destructive Art: Demonstration by G. Metzger*, South Bank Manifesto, and contains reprints of the 1st and 2nd manifestos. It was printed in an edtion of 1000, and given out at the South Bank on 3 July 1961. (A black line under the title) actually deletes the reference to the IUA Congress.

1962

4th Manifesto: *Manifesto World*, 7 October 1962. Published as *Manifesto World* London,1962. Single sheet. 'Machine, Auto-Creative, & Auto-Destructive Art', *Ark, Journal of the Royal College of Art* (London), no. 32, Summer 1962. Illustrations.

1963

Centre for Advanced Creative Studies, London 1963. Joint statement with Marcello Salvadori on the aims of the centre, together with 'Research in Dimensions and Raw Industrial Material' by Marcello Salvadori, and 'Theory and Practice of Auto-Destructive Art and Auto-Creative Art' by G.M. Broadsheet.

1964

5th Manifesto: *On Random Activity in Material/Transforming Works of Art*, 30 July 1964. Published in 'Four Manifestos by Gustav Metzger.' *Signals: Newsbulletin of the Centre for Advanced Creative Study London* vol. 1, no. 2, September 1964. (Subtitle of Signals changes with no. 3 – see also *ICA Bulletin*, April 1964.) (First publication of the 5th and final manifesto – here titled number 'IV'. Accompanied by reprints of 1st, 2nd and 3rd manifestos.) Illustrations.

'With the five bubble machines…'. *Signals*, vol. 1, no. 2, September 1964. Statement on David Medalla.

1965

Auto-Destructive Art: Metzger at AA, ACC, London, June 1965. ('Expanded version of a talk given at the Architectural Association on 24 February, 1965'. ACC was an independent student press at the A.A. Edition of 200.)

Auto-Destructive Art: Metzger at AA, Destruction/Creation, London, October 1965. (Reprint of the text first published by the ACC in June, plus photographs and reprints of all five manifestos. Destruction/Creation means self-published. Edition of 1000.)

'Auto-Destructive Art', *Granta*, Cambridge, 6 November 1965. (The title should have been 'The Chemical Revolution in Art'.) Illustrations.

1966

Art of Liquid Crystals, London, 1966. Single sheet.

'The Possiblilty of Auto-Destructive Architecture', *Clip-Kit: Studies in Environmental Design* (Independent student publication at the Architectural Association, London), no. 2, 1966.

'Auto-Destructive Art', *Anarchy*, no. 64, June 1966. (Letter to the editor in response to a report of the 1965 Architectural Association talk and demonstration in *Anarchy* no. 61, March 1966.)

'Gustav Metzger', *Art and Artists* (London) vol. 1, no. 5, August 1966. (In special 'Auto-Destructive' issue, editor Mario Amaya, assistant editor Kenneth Coutts-Smith.) Illustrations.

'An Overwhelming Concern with Shelter!', *Peace News*, London, 2 September 1966.

DIAS Resurgence, London, vol. 1, no. 4, November/ December 1966.

Introduction to 'Excerpts from Selected Papers Presented at the 1966 Destruction in Art Symposium', *Studio International*, London, December 1966.

1967

DIAS Preliminary Report, DIAS, London, February 1967.

'Manifest 1961', 'Briefe von Gustav Metzger an Wolf Vostell', 'DIAS Preliminary Report', *dé-coll/age*, Köln, no. 6, July 1967. (The South Bank Manifesto. Also includes photographs.)

DIAS-Information, London, no. 1, March 1967, no. 2, June 1967, no. 3, August 1967, no. 4, September 1967, no. 5, March 1968. Single sheets with graphics.

1968

Arts Festival '68, University College of Swansea, Extremes Touch, Swansea, 1968. Single sheet. Outline of the exhibition.

'Five Screens With Computer', Jasia Reichardt (ed.), *Cybernetic Serendipity: the Computer and the Arts*, London: Studio International, London, 1968. Text, and sketch of the activity of the screens.

1969

'Automata in History', parts 1 and 2, *Studio International*, London, March and October 1969. (Photocopy reprint of part one issued on the occasion of the Computer Arts Society's *Event One*, Royal College of Art, London, 29–30 March 1969.)

'Five Screens With Computer (1963–69)', *Event One*, Computer Arts Society, London, 1969. Text, and computer graphic of one screen. Catalogue.

Notes on the Crisis in Technological Art London, 1969. Given out at the 'post-mortem on Event One' at the British Computer Society, 3 April 1969. Single sheet.

PAGE: Bulletin of the Computer Arts Society, London: editor from 1969–72. The first issue has a signed comment on *Event One*.

'Zagreb Manifesto' (with Jonathan Benthall and Gordon Hyde), *Studio International*, June 1969. (Included in 'News and Notes', p. 259.)

'Statements', *Circuit*, no. 10/11, London 1969. Artists' statements including one by G.M.

'Theory of Auto-Destructive Art' (Catalogue for the Anti-University, 1968). Course description.

1970

'Five Screens with Computer' and 'Design Studies...' *Tendencije 4: Zagreb, 1968–1969* (Computers and Visual Research), Zagreb, Galerija Suvremene Umjetnosti, 1970. (Catalogue of exhibition, 5 May-30 June 1969). Texts and illustrations; computer graphics with D.E. Evans, Beverly Rowe, A.W. Nutbourne, and R.J. Stibbs; model – all relating to *Five Screens With Computer*.

Do You Eat?, University of London, Slade School of Fine Art, London, February 1970. Single sheet.

'Kinetics', *Art & Artists*, London, September 1970.

'Social Responsibility and the Computer Professional: The Rise of an Idea in America. Part 1', *PAGE: Bulletin of the Computer Arts Society*, no. 11, London, October 1970, Includes bibliography. (There were no further parts).

International Coalition for the Liquidation of Art, London, 15 October 1970. Single sheet.

'Notes on the Crisis in Technological Art' and 4 Manifestos by Gustav Metzger', *Klepht*, no. 1, Swansea, January 1970. (Reprints of 'Notes...', and 1st, 2nd, 3rd, and 5th manifestos.)

New Ideas in Plotter Design Construction and Output, London, 1970. This is the second paper presented at *Computer Graphics 70* and formed part of the proceedings, but is not included in the book. Illustrations.

'Five Screens With Computer: Computer Graphic Aspects of a Sculpture Project', *Computer Graphics 70*, Plenum Press, London, 1971.

'Sculpture with Power', A. Alono Concheiro (ed.), *Memoria de la Conferencia Internacional sobre Sistemas, Redes y Computadoras*, Mexico, 1971.

Udo Kultermann, *Art-Events & Happenings*, Mathews Miller Dunbar, London, 1971. (New York edition is titled *Art & Life*, Tübingen edition, *Leben und Kunst*. Each reproduces the South Bank Manifesto.)

'Untitled Paper on Theme Number Three', *Bit International* (Zagreb) no. 7, 1971. (Also includes 'Zagreb Manifesto') *Dialogue with the Machine*, Boris Keleman and Radoslav Putar (eds.), Bit International and Galerije Grade, Zagreb, 1971.

1972

'A Critical Look at Artist Placement Group', *Studio International*, London, January 1972.

Joseph Beuys, *Information Action*. Transcript of the soundtrack of a video-tape of Beuys' action at the Tate Gallery, 25 February 1972, which includes an exchange between G.M. and Beuys. Tate Gallery Archive: TAV 616AB.

'Second Floor…', *Newsheet: Gallery House London*, no. 1, 1972. Text outlining G.M. exhibition, plus plan of show. Single sheet.

'Stockholm June: ein projek für Stockholm 1–15 Juni 1972.' *documenta 5*, Verlag Dokumenta/Bertelsmann Verlag, Kassel, 1972. Text, illustration of model, and ground plan for projected work by G.M.

Executive Profile, London, 1972. Single sheet issued by the Institute of Contemporary Arts, London. (Draft in the Tate Gallery Archive).

'Notes on Recent Work', and 'Projects for 'British Thing' show', *Prismavis*, Høvikkoden, no. 4, Norway, September 1972. Illustration.

'From the City Pages', *Studio International*, London, December 1972.

1974

Untitled statements, illustrations and 'The Art Dealer: a Bibliography', *Art into Society/Society into Art: Seven German Artists*, Institute of Contemporary Arts, London, 1974 (catalogue).

'Art in Germany under National Socialism', *Studio International*, London, March/April 1976.

Andrew Brighton and Lynda Morris, (eds.), *Towards Another Picture: an anthology of Writings by Artists Working in Britain 1945–1977*, Midland Group, Nottingham, 1977. (Includes extracts from several texts by G.M.)

1981

Faschismus Deutschland: Darstellung, Analyse, Bekämpfen. Two sheets in the loose-leaf catalogue: Vor dem Abbruch, Kunstmuseum, Bern, 1981.

Kollektiv Cordula Frowein, Gustav Metzger, Klaus Staeck Passiv-Explosiv/…Pressegespräch, Köln, 1981. Single printed sheet.

Passiv-Explosiv: Entwurf einer Ausstellung, Köln, 1981. Two printed sheets.

1984

Press Release: Artists Support Peace, January 6th 1983, London, 1983. Single sheet. (Incorrectly dated: should read 1984.)

Thomas Kellein *'Fröhliche Wissenschaft': Das Archiv Sohm*, Staatsgalerie, Stuttgart, 1986. (Reproduces the South Bank Manifesto, and a late draft for the 1st Manifesto. Note errata slip.)

1990

Wiener Aktionismus 1960-1974, Studio Oggetto, Milano, 1990. Folded printed sheet.

1992

Earth Minus Environment: a Sculptural Project for the Earth Summit, Rio de Janeiro, 1–12 June 1992, Amsterdam, 6 January 1992. Single sheet.

1993

David Mellor, *The Sixties Art Scene in London*, Phaidon, London, 1993.
(Reproduces the South Bank Manifesto, also reprints the first three manifestos, amongst other writings).

1994

Elements Centre, Amsterdam, 1994. Single sheet.

1995

Untitled text, Martin Caiger-Smith (ed.), *Yves Klein Now: Sixteen Views*, South Bank Centre, London, 1995. Published on the occasion of the exhibition *Yves Klein: Leap into the Void* at the Hayward Gallery, 9 February–23 April 1995.

1996

Gustav Metzger:'Damaged Nature, Auto-Destructive Art', with an essay by Andew Wilson and a chronology and bibliography by Clive Phillpot, Coracle @ workfortheeyetodo, London, 1996. Illustrated.

Earth to Galaxies: On Destruction and Destructivity, Pavel Büchler and Charles Esche (eds.), foreword by Ross Birrell, Tramline No.5, Glasgow, 1996.

Artist's statement, *Life/Live*, Bossé, Lawrence (ed), Musée d'Art Moderne de la Ville de Paris, Paris 1996.

1997

Gustav Metzger: Manifeste Schriften Konzepte, Luise Metzel (ed.), foreword by Justin Hoffmann, translations by Andrea Stumpf, Verlag Silke Schreiber, Munich, 1997.

1998

'The Artist in the Eye of the Storm', John Wood (ed.), *The Virtual Embodied*, Routledge, London, 1998.

'The Artist in the Face of Social Collapse', Melanie Keen (ed.), *Frequencies: Investigations into Culture History and Technology*, Institute of International Visual Arts, London, 1998.

Selected Bibliography, Films and Videos

Arrowsmith, Pat, 'Auto-Destructive Art', *Peace News*, London, 22 July 1993.

Art In Europe Since 1945, BBC TV, February 1969 (Nancy Thomas/Paul Overy).

Art Spectrum London, Alexandra Palace, London,1971 (catalogue).

Art and Artists, 'Auto-Destructive' issue, vol. 1, no. 5, London, August 1966.

Auto-Destructive Art, The Activities of G. Metzger, film, 15 mins., (director) Harold Liversidge, London, 1963.

Bann, Stephen, *Experimental Painting: construction, abstraction, destruction, reduction*, London/New York, 1970.

Bann, Stephen, Reg Gadney, Frank Popper and Phil Steadman, *4 Essays on Kinetic Art*, London, 1966.

Benthall, Jonathan, 'Art and Technology', *Studio International*, London, May 1969.

Bewogen, Beweging, Stedelijk Museum, Amsterdam, 1961/Museum Louisiana, Humlebaek/*Roerelse i Konsten*, Moderna Museet, Stockholm (catalogue).

Blackburn, Susan, 'If You Had £200 To Spend On Art' (Mario Amaya)', *Weekend Telegraph*, London, 10 June 1966.

Bossé, Laurence and Hans Ulrich Obrist, *Life/Live*, 2 vols., Musée d'Art Moderne de la Ville de Paris, Paris, 1996 (catalogue).

Brighton, Andrew and Lynda Morris (eds.), *Towards another picture. An anthology of writings by artists working in Britain*, 1945–1977, Nottingham, 1977.

Bullock, Alan and Oliver Stallybrass, *Fontana Dictionary of Modern Thought*, London, 1977.

Bullock, Michael, 'Cardboards arranged by Gustav Metzger', *Art News & Review*, London, 21 November 1959.

Chilvers, Ian (ed.), *A Dictionary of 20th Century Art*, Oxford, 1998.

Cork, Richard, *David Bomberg*, London/New Haven, 1987.

Davis, Douglas: *Art into Future*, London, 1973 (U.S. edition: *Art & the Future*).

Diest, Antje van, *Gustav Metzger: London Art in the Sixties*, Leiden University, 1992.

documenta 5, Kassel, 1972 (catalogue).

Freeman, Alan, 'The truth about our generation', *Rave*, London, February 1966.

Gamboni, Dario, *The Destruction of Art: Iconaclasm and Vandalism since the French Revolution*, London, 1997.
Gimpel, Jean, *The Cult of Art*, London, 1969.

Glew, Adrian, 'The Mad Messiah...', *Don't Tell It*, London, October 1995.

Goldberg, Roselee, *Performance*, Thames and Hudson, London, 1998.

Hansen, Al, 'London: Destruction in Art Symposium', *Arts Magazine*, New York, November 1966.

Henri, Adrian, *Environments and Happenings*, London, 1974 (U.S. edition: *Total Art: Environments*, Happenings and Performance, New York/Toronto, 1974).

Hewison, Robert, *Too Much: Art and Society in the Sixties*, London, 1987.

Hoffmann, Justin, 'Gustav Metzger und die autodestruktive Kunst', *Artis*, no. 5, Bern, May, 1991.

Hoffmann, Justin, *Destruktionskunst. Der Mythos der Zerstörung in der Kunst der frühen sechziger Jahre*, München, 1995.

Home, Stewart, *The Assault on Culture*, London, 1988.

Houédard, Dom Sylvester, 'The Aesthetics of the Death Wish', *Art and Artists*, London, August 1966. Expanded version: *The Aesthetics of the Death Wish*, Destruction/Creation, London, 1966

Joachimides, Christos and Norman Rosenthal, *Art into Society/Society into Art*, ICA London, London, 1974 (catalogue).

Kultermann, Udo, *The New Painting*, London, 1969

Mellor, David, *The Sixties Art Scene in London*, London, 1993.

'Miles interviews Pete Townshend', *International Times*, London, 13 February 1967.

Naylor, Colin and Genesis P. Orridge (eds.), *Contemporary Artists*, London/New York/Chicago, 1977.
Nuttall, Jeff, *Bomb Culture*, London, 1968.

Obrist, Hans Ulrich, Video Interview with Gustav Metzger, London, November 1997.

Oxlade, Roy, *David Bomberg and the Borough. An Approach to Drawing*, Royal College of Art, MA dissertation, 2 vols., London, 1976.

Plagemann, Stephen, 'Auto-Destructive Art', *Sinistra*, Cambridge, 1965.

Popper, Frank, *The relationships of auto-destructive and auto-creative art and kinetic art*, unpublished, January, 1966.

Popper, Frank, *Origins & Development in Kinetic Art*, London/Greenwich, 1968.

Prosser, John, 'Photoreport on DIAS', *Art and Artists*, London, October 1966.

Reichard, Jasia, 'The Art of Suicide', *Time & Tide*, London, 25 June 1960.

Reichard, Jasia, *The Computer in Art*, London, 1971.

Rydon, John, 'It's Pictures from Packing Cases', *Daily Express*, London, 12 November, 1959.

Rydon, John, 'Modern Art will fall to bits', *Daily Express*, London, 15 March 1960.

Schimmel, Paul (ed.), *Out of Actions: between performance and the object*, 1949–1978, MOCA, Los Angeles, 1998.

Schönberger, Angela, 'Art in Germany under National Socialism', *Kritische Berichte*, no.1, Giessen, 1977.

Stiles, Kristine and Peter Selz (eds.), *Theories and Documents of Contemporary Art: a sourcebook of artists' writings*, Berkley/Los Angeles/London, 1996.

Seitz, William C., *Art in the Age of Aquarius 1955–1970*, Washington, 1992.

Sohm, Hanns, *Happening & Fluxus*, Köln, 1970.

Stiles, Kristine, *The Destruction in Art Smposium (DIAS): The Radical Cultural Project of Event-Structured Live Art*, PhD thesis, University of California, Berkeley, 1987.

Stiles, Kristine, 'Selected Comments on Destruction Art', *Boek voor de Instabiele Media*, s'Hertogenbosch, 1992.

Stiles, Kristine, 'Uncorrupted Joy: *International Art Actions', Out of Actions: Between performance and the object, 1949–1979*, Paul Schimmel (ed.), Los Angeles, 1998.

Strauss, Herbert A. and Werner Röder, *International Biographical Dictionary of Central European Emigrés, 1933–1945*, vol. 2, part 2, München/New York/London/Paris,1983.

Turner, Jane (ed.), *The Dictionary of Art*, 34 vols., London, 1996. (See entries: 'Auto-Destructive Art', vol. 2 and 'Gustav Metzger', vol. 21.)

Walker, John A., *Glossary of Art, Architecture & Design Since 1945*, 3rd edition, London, 1993.

Walker, John A., 'Art & Anarchism', *Art & Artists*, London, May 1978.

Walker, John A., *John Latham: the incidental person: his art and ideas*, London, 1995.

Walker, John A., 'Message from the Margin', *Art Monthly*, London, October 1995.

Williams, Emmett, *My Life in Flux – and Vice Versa*, Stuttgart, 1991.

Wilson, Andrew, 'Telling it Like it Really Wasn't', *Art Monthly*, London, May 1993.

Wilson, Andrew, 'Life v Art', *Art Monthly*, London, November 1996.

Wilson, Andrew, Video Interview with Gustav Metzger, London, January 1998.

Wilson, Andrew, 'Papa what did you do when the nazis built the concentration camps? My dear, they never told us anything'.
Gustav Metzger. Damaged Nature, Auto-Destructive Art, London, 1966.